My MENOPAUSE
My Journal
My Rules

My menopause, My Journal, My Rules
Copyright © 2023 Victoria Hardy
All rights reserved.
Cover & book design by Davina Hopping
No part of this book can be reproduced in any form or by written, electronic or mechanical, including photocopying, recording, or by any information retrieval system without written permission in writing by the author.

Published by Rebellious Ink

Printed by Book Printing UK www.bookprintinguk.com
Remus House, Coltsfoot Drive, Peterborough, PE2 9BF

Printed in Great Britain
Although every precaution has been taken in the preparation of this book, the publisher and author assume no responsibility for errors or omissions. Neither is any liability assumed for damages resulting from the use of information contained herein.
ISBN 978-1-7392783-0-4

For Grace & The Boy

This is for you,

To open the doors just a little more

for your generation...

and remember, we all have it in us to make shit happen!

xxx

contents.

9
Hey From Me
A little introduction to why I'm here

15
Getting The Most Out of This Book
Say hello to the experts, understand the power of journaling, tackle inclusive language and you'll find your instructions on how you'll write your own rules.

23
RULE 1
Connect To Your Wellbeing
The definition of Wellbeing explained and how you discover what it means for you

29
RULE 2
Understand These Menopause Shenanigans
Menopause stages explained along with enough symptoms you can shake a stick at

41
RULE 3
Journal, Track, Journal Some More
3 Months of journal to track symptoms, feelings and gratitude.

69
RULE 4
Get The Medical Stuff In Order
Prep like a pro for any appointments, HRT and the alternatives, make appointment notes and avoid Medical Gaslighting

97
RULE 5
Be Well Prepped For 'The No Ovary Club'
Get prepped for surgery, plan post-op self care, or learn what it's like for those who've waved goodbye to their uterus, including Sophie in her 20s.

117
RULE 6
Love Your Body
Covering sleep (or lack of), fueling our bodies, how we move, breathe and check our boobs! Amy shares her story and of course from hot flushes to loving the skin we're in...oh, and tackling hair we want and hair we don't

143
RULE 7
Start A Re-Vulva-Lution
Get acquainted with yourself, delve literally into the power of self pleasure to tackle low sex drive before moving onto pelvic health.

177
RULE 8
Soothe Your Messy Mind
Losing yourself with the mental symptoms is soothed with finding ways to help stress, overwhelm, anxiety and panic attacks, ready to build confidence and create space for joy. The ups and downs of brain fog and you get to literally rip out some rages! Read Gayle's poem and explore Meditation, Mindfulness and sitting in the Mess.

229
RULE 9
Find What Your Soul Needs

Get in flow with all things energy, starting with a history lesson. Claim back your connection to self, learn not to give a fuck with a little ritual and tap into manifesting, create your vision and action your goals. Helping you move into your Queen-hood

259
RULE 10
Enlighten Your Loved Ones

Open up the conversations with partners, friends and the kids. Natasha tells us her teenage experience to help us feel bolder. We ponder 'do the guys really get it?' Whilst giving a thought to same sex couples too. Sam tells her experience with her partner and there's a letter for yours to read to help the conversation along.

279
RULE 11

It starts with our own stigma before moving on to talking at work and Claire shares how she flooded a boardroom! Looking after yourself as your own boss or if you're studying, I've got you, and Sheree gives some words of wisdom and she hit Menopause at 7! We take a pause to grieve and hear about transgender, manopause, post menopause, cultural impact and how disability plays a role, all from voices of those who have experienced it first hand.

Crushing The Taboo In Society

313
RULE 12
Create Change

Reflect on the impact you can make for yourself and for further generations, spurred on by words from menopause campaigner and legend herself Diane Danzebrink, write down your own plan of attack to crush the taboo around you.

321
THE ULTIMATE RULE
Always Remember You're a Badass Queen!

Write a letter to yourself with kindness and a final farewell from me.

329
THE LITTLE EXTRAS...

Places to go for help, community, all the activity pages you need and a shout out to those that helped make this book possible

INTERVAL OF EVENTS

Throughout mixed amongst my stories are these little nuggets of the present, happening while I wrote this, I am truly living this with you as you read.

My Menopause, My Journal, My Rules!

hey you
welcome TO THE
madness

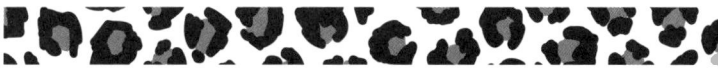

SO, WHY ARE YOU HERE?

Before the formal introductions begin I'd love you to think about the reason why this book has found its way into your hands. Maybe you want to feel more connected to others, perhaps it's part of discovering more about this time in your life and what it means to you, or simply you're curious to learn a few things.

We often don't take time for ourselves through life in general, yet here you are, things are changing and you've been called to pick this up...why?

I'd love you to write a few words here, make a note of your reasons, maybe how you're feeling right now? There's no wrong or right way. It will be a beautiful thing to reflect on when you've reached the final pages.

. . . .

. . . .

. . . .

. . . .

. . . .

. . . .

. . . .

Let's get into it

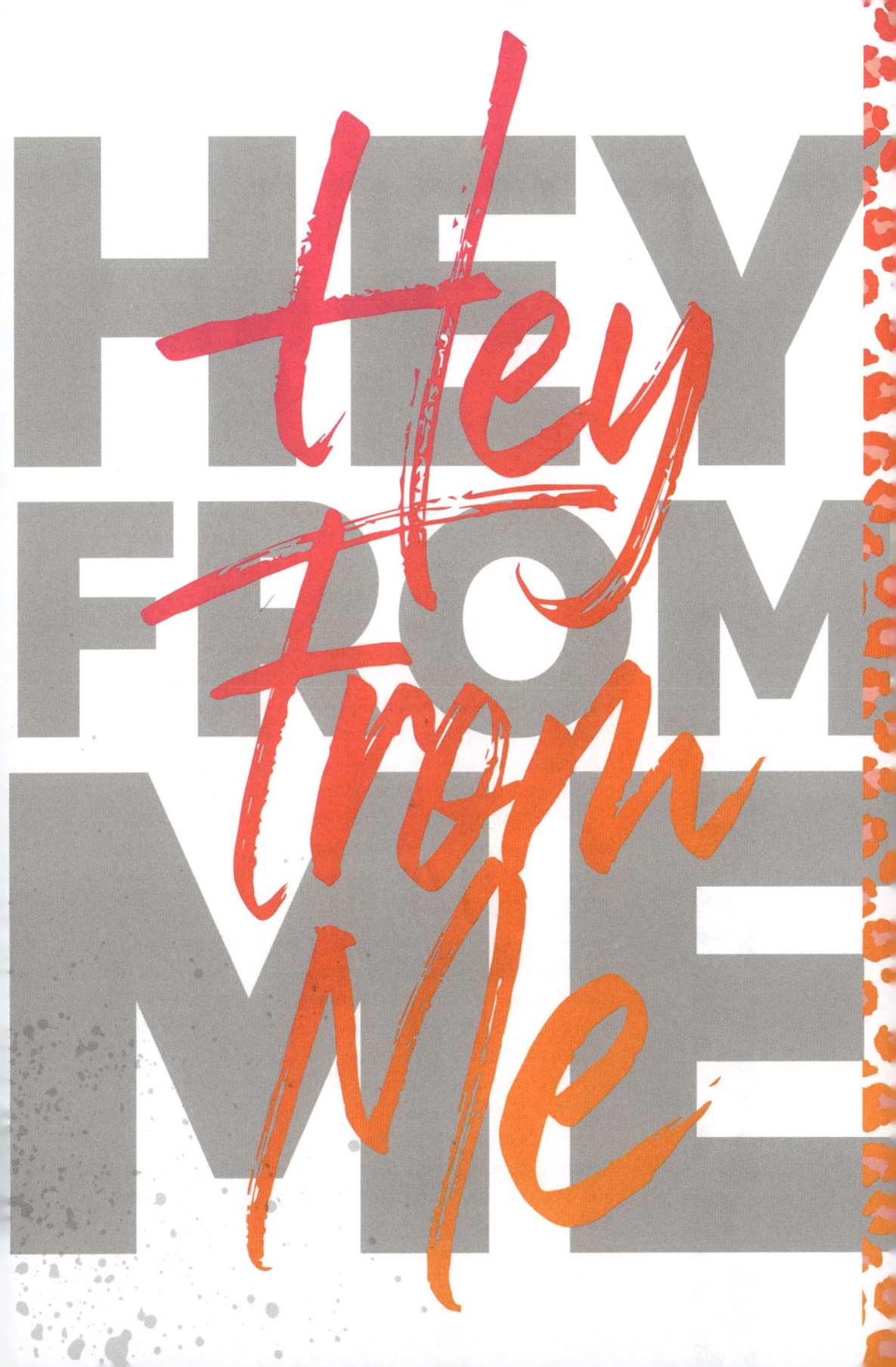

'YOUR UTERUS IS TOUCHING YOUR SPINE,' HE SAID...

Don't you know who I am? You don't? Exactly! I'm just a thirty something gal, a bit of a badass, a bit of a mess, trying to live my life through a rather earlier than expected menopause. My celeb status spans as far as being in the TV crowd during 'Children in Need' at the age of seven. I wasn't even holding one of those fat cheques! My 'Pudsy Bear' ears sat on what can only be described as a 'mushroom haircut' looking a bit of a twat! The child modelling career never worked out, so nowadays the day job hits the bank account, the mortgage goes out as I manage to just about fill up my car and the remaining pennies get sucked away to endless kids clubs and taxiing teenagers around. This leaves my overdraft to subsidize anything that helps me pull my big girl pants up and get through these menopause shenanigans.

Hopeful, as I hit my thirties, that sleepless nights, squabbles and wanting to throw Mr Tumble out of the window were over, we'd move into a more *we've got our life together*, boho, globally travelled type of foursome, like we'd drowned in Pinterest. We're mightily imperfect our unit of four: 'The Hubs' (not *that* Mr Hardy...we can only imagine), the fierce and mighty 'Sloth-teen' and 'The Boy'... the kid we attached to an extending dog lead as he speedily balance-biked along the promenade, like a two-year-old 'Evil Knievel!'. They'd all fought their way through their own battles; from premature births, concussions, knocked teeth and underfoot midnight Lego, to them all seeing me in severe pain, toddler eyes onlooking as my vagina erupted in public loos like a vampire spewing. They'd been there through my endless hospital visits and operations, helping me recover with careful cuddles.

Now I was the big 3-0 and adulting was under the belt, it was our time to fill the passports, consider, for less than a minute, homeschooling (ironic to write post covid) and for a while this new decade of living seemed like it was going to go our way.

Just a couple of years in, my chronic illness of Endometriosis flared its nasty wrath. The procedures weren't working and the pain struck, reaching almost every part of my body. With risks that no-one wants to hear, it was time...the hysterectomy talk was happening. After eighteen procedures since the age of fifteen my body was battered, and as I glared at the MRI scan, my consultant announced, 'Your uterus is touching your spine and there's an extremely high risk of at least three cancers.' He continued: 'I can see you're exhausted from pain and it's likely your bowel is damaged. So what do you want to do?' He stared at me waiting for an answer. It took me approximately 0.3 seconds to respond, almost gleefully,

'let's get it all out'.

Eleven months later through keyhole surgery I had a full hysterectomy (remaining ovary and tube, uterus, cervix the lot). I was thirty-four... job done I thought!

Being thrown into surgical menopause at that age not only hit me like a knockout punch in the face but I was also unaware of what the hell was actually happening. What the surgery entailed – the risks, the importance of rest and the acute focus on no more children – was the agenda of all medical conversations. Chatting through what happens after or support I'd need for the shit I'd wade through for possibly the next two decades of my life, was...well, a bit flaky.

Since my operation, there's been the very highs of being out of twenty years of physical pain from Endometriosis, Adenomyosis (feel free to search the web) and the constant huge rupturing cysts, to the crushing lows of the mental and physical disruption that followed with surgical menopause.

My hormones have caused utter havoc, crushing my confidence, stealing my personality away to the point where I almost signed out of this beautiful world altogether – and what an awful shame that would have been.

Hey From Me

However, a lot of healing has happened since then and yes, at times my menopause is still messy, but I promise you it's not all been tears and tantrums. I really want you to know that straight up, before you put this book in the freezer and go and hide behind the sofa.

They just didn't teach us this menopause shizzle at school, or in adult life for that matter, so I wasn't clued up! Here I was, suddenly being some sort of millennial in the middle. Stuck in-between generations born before, who kept their mouths tightly shut, and those that post their farts in jars on the internet, who are quite frankly having conversations way earlier. I needed to learn from my elders, but they were no-where to be seen, and yet I want to help the generations to come who expect more in terms of openness, inclusivity, equality and support. I didn't want others to feel quite so out on a dimply limb like I did and figured – although certainly less taboo than it once was – maybe I could bridge a bit of a gap around this menopause stuff? Especially for those of us 'out of the statistical norm' that don't often get a mention in the conversation at all. **So here I am!**

I'M WINGING IT.

I've tried all sorts and learned, along with this turbulent ride, there's a beautiful connection to self that happens, acting like a portal to step up into what you're really capable of. **Helping you see that is where my strength lies.**

Because what I am is a conversationalist through spoken and written words. I'll go there, saying the thing that's a little uncomfortable or 'ick', if it helps us learn more about ourselves and each other.

I once described to my daughter how a vulva was different to a vagina over a curry at the local Indian restaurant, creatively using a glass a beer bottle and a napkin; and yes, it was a family meal for my mother's seventy-sixth birthday!

Important note!

I'm no celeb influencer (not yet anyway), wonder woman activist, medical professional or MP. No menopause Guru or Doula (oh blimey, I'll put money on someone coining menopause Doula soon)! I couldn't even tell you all the names of the Hormone Replacement Therapies (HRT) I've tried and really have no interest in being able to properly pronounce every single medical term surrounding this topic.

When Mum uttered the words, 'shh, the man over on that table might overhear you,' I simply replied loudly, 'well his wife might be quite pleased...at least he'll learn where a clitoris is!' She looked at me with her 'did you really just say that?' eyes and continued to tuck into her poppadom.

I advocate for better in my own little way, from dancing trends mixed with voice notes in DMs on social media, to writing deeply and speaking vulnerably to help others. I believe creating a community is where it's at.

There's also the acute understanding that **menopause is not a fad and shouldn't be treated as so.**

The media awareness is great and the general menopause conversation is starting to blossom, yet somehow I'm left still feeling underrepresented and see so many gaps in the conversation, it kind of makes my hormones rage and my rant pants get pulled up for those who don't have a voice! Because, like you, I'm just *living* it, learning how to navigate through and find my way. So, I'm here to bring a bit of realness through the times it feels like a shit show, whilst helping you feel like you can connect back to yourself. Because believe me, it's easy to get lost in the jargon, the statistics and the science, and stop listening to what's within us.

In here I share some things I've tried, liked, loved and loathed. We'll dabble with thoughts about those that came before us, share stories of those in it now and I get a bit poetic too. These things are *all* in their way helping me step into — what I've heard and quite like to quote – my 'Queen-hood', finding my *own* rules for it all.

So, this is a kind of conversation with others *and* yourself all in one, that might just make your experience of this menopause thing a little more 'yours'. Whether you're in the thick of it or tinkering on the edge about to embark.

We are not withered or past it,
We won't hide how beautifully human we are.
We sit together in the difficult,
Share as we adapt and lift each other to stand tall.
To be more fierce than we were before.

My Menopause, My Journal, My Rules!

Being yourself is a fucking Superpower!

Who you are... is beautiful

Don't get too excited but I've got a handful of people that are super duper in their field to add their thoughts where necessary. However, it was intentional that there's not a doctor in sight... This book isn't about to give you *everything* you need to know: all the facts, stats, in-depth opinions or scientific hoo ha's... **why?**

Sciencey Thoughts...

- Because those books are already written, out there and marvellous.
- You can Google
- Your actual doctor is the one to seek or sometimes challenge over medical advice.
- Statistics quickly go out of date and I'm not sure my Estrogen levels have the capacity to keep updating this every time someone leaves the workplace, or they change their thinking about whether HRT should be free!
- I'm pants at science...although I do look great in white.

Finally, and most importantly, this is about you, because it's

your menopause

so it should be

your rules!

It will be beautifully messy in a different way to mine, so take my part with a pinch of spicy and use this to write what

you need.

OWN IT!

That's how you're going to

Getting The Most Out of This Book

17

THE POWER OF JOURNALING

Journaling was one of things that literally saved me, honestly it was a game changer! When I lost myself through this hormonal fuckery it felt like my mind was not my own. If losing my shit was a sport I would have entered the Olympics and taken the gold. My head was so full, I had little space to get through a day without feeling like the spinning plates of home and work, along with trying to understand my body and who I was supposed to be were not only wobbling, but cracking like worn out crockery. Until one day it smashed to smithereens around me — like the remnants of a whopping great Greek party.

I then started to write stuff down as it helped me organise, brain-dump, learn what was going on physically and (on very dark days) fantasize about how many different ways I could bury anyone that left washing on the floor — don't worry I've shared these tips later! I still journal using the bullet method and feel disorganised or not particularly in control if I miss a few days. I've found over the years it's been a mix of thoughts, lists, important dates, medical info, cathartic poetry and raucous rambles. Along with doodles, goals and gratitude, even tear the page out rages! I love it and really believe it's healing, so I wanted to bring this cleansing purge element to the menopause party for you.

There's plenty of wellness journals out there that offer a consistent page on page approach and if ticking off how many glasses of water you've drunk, or depressingly colouring in that half hour you've slept rocks your world, knock your socks off. This isn't one of those books!

This journal, much like menopause, is not consistent. It keeps you on your toes, only having to commit to repetition where absolutely needed. You have 12 + 1 rules for ease, nudging you to seek what works for you. This will help you determine your own set of empowering rules. **making your menopause your own.**

For the record it's not a guide either, because it's not my job to guide you through. It's kind of your job. I know, someone's playing devil's advocate, right? It's a risky move for me to say this but however you feel right now, however much information gets thrown at you, if you choose to stay stagnant and not own this time yourself, then going in circles will be your vibe. This is something to comfort you as you get to grips with what you truly need in your menopause, as you build a freakin' empire of your rules and make it yours.

However, yours doesn't mean yours alone. Because in a world where menopause, along with mental health, is somewhat still taboo, the things I missed were connection to others and feeling like I belonged somewhere in the thick of my symptoms. Most of the time I had little knowledge of what was happening and who could help. I felt (like many of us) that I didn't fit into the traditional box that society labels as 'menopausal'. Move over grey hair, baggy tights and cardigans! The thing is, outside the historic patriarchal and media world of 'woman of a certain age, dried up, going through the change,' lingo, there isn't a box for menopause. It's time to shake things up.

We all experience it differently, but none of us want to feel on our own. So yes, your rules, your menopause, but as you make your way through I'm here to hold your hand, in a non-creepy way!

As you turn the pages, I hope you feel more connected to yourself, me, her, them, they, him and the others amongst us that are *all* feeling what you may be too. These pages are for you and within them there are spaces for you to scribble, write and tear out. There's useful stuff to read over, think about and even do, all amongst stories you might connect to, learn from and hopefully pass on through conversations, keeping these important messages of menopause moving.

IT'S NOT ALL ABOUT WOMEN — SORRY, NOT SORRY

Although I've used the words woman/women/her/she for ease throughout, I know that menopause does not discriminate. I'm not dis-empowering women with this sentiment but empowering all. Please know that *everyone* was part of my thinking as I wrote, not just women but Trans men and Trans women, non-binary peeps and all those in-between. Part of us learning about ourselves is also learning about others' experiences too, a different perspective from the comfort of our own. Although I'm sure I have left gaps, these aren't intentional, I'm merely finding my way. But I hope you'll take a little something away to help open a conversation you might not have had before and stay open minded with me. You'll make your own pathway through this time in your life and feel badass again, all whilst making menopause a bit more bloody normal for everyone!

Menopause has no **age, gender, or culture.** it affects *or* indirectly *affects us* all.

Getting The Most Out of This Book

OH, FFS THERE'S INSTRUCTIONS!

Firstly, you're going to need a pen.

- 👑 Please bend, write inside, rip out, take along to medical appointments too. In fact, do everything we're usually told not to do to a book! And yep, I'll be happy with the 'bottom of the bag grime' on the cover!

- 👑 There's no wrong that can be written. Scribbling and crossing out are allowed, as is adding notes, extra paper, stapled or sticky taped. If it helps to keep it all in one place…then do!

- 👑 Be open-minded. Some of the activities (oh blimey she added activities) might feel a bit woah or woo, or just 'erm does she really think I'm going to do or write that?' Give it a go before you decide what you do and don't like. That even goes for the things I didn't get on with, they might be right up your street.

- 👑 I encourage you to read all the sections, you may enjoy the stories or pass on the tips even if they don't feel directly relevant to you personally.

- 👑 We've established I love a swear word. Yes, there's colourful language throughout. Let's not add another taboo of swearing to the long list we have to deal with already. But I'm also deep, intuitive, spiritual and poetic. I'll share that side too, lean into this.

- 👑 There's no order. Transforming and levelling up is messy, so go to the sections you need when you need them.

- 👑 Please be honest - with yourself, your words and thoughts…it's powerful stuff when you can tap into that.

- 👑 Okay so I'm going to ask you to reach around the back and check your rear end. I'm talking about the books 'Little Extras' section, before your mind wonders to some weird self-diagnostic probing! You should find a few things neatly inserted within the pages, ready to write, rip out and burn and somewhere to scream out your rages or plan revenge! You'll need these when prompted and there's contacts for if you need support too.

- ♛ To yourself - be kind! Menopause is *allowed* to feel like a big deal. Sometimes it's grief-filled, painful and mind fumbling. Sometimes it's freedom, relief and wisdom. However it comes your way or affects you, I've got you. Until, fingers and flaps crossed, you're in a place where you no longer need this little friend on your person because you'll feel like you're owning it. Putting one foot in front of the other a little more sturdily, empowered to speak up, advocate and share your experience. It might just come a bit more naturally after working to re-write the rules, not just for yourself but helping others to do the same.

Enjoy Peeps!

Victoria ♡

Know that as you hold this, as you read these words... there are others doing the same, winging it through, just as you are — and they have got you too.

WELLNESS IS NOT LINEAR

RULE 1

Connect to your wellbeing

Before we really kick off let's just clarify this word 'wellbeing'. It's often waved around more than my fan mid-hot-flush in the heat of the London Underground, and oh, how we get smothered in the latest active wear, self-care fad, or how many digits are topping up on our wrists. We forget what its real definition is...

It's subjective. It's how you individually experience and evaluate the choices you make and how you live your time on this planet. In other words, your own wellbeing only really feels, or in fact is, in good shape if it's aligned to you personally.

Wellbeing in its purest form is about your quality of life.

There's so much out there telling us how we need to achieve a good level of wellness. But when do we stop and think about what we actually need? Or look inside ourselves to understand what quality of life means to us? This is a time to delve into your own quality of life in a way that speaks to you.

Looking at and leaning into what makes you feel well is ever changing. It's multi-faceted and complicated because as humans we're all of those wonderful things. I could never cover everything that you should be seeking out, trying, or letting go of during this time, we're complex beings and although sometimes it's the simplest of things that help the most, only we can do the doing, make the changes and be curious about what makes us feel better. Then we'll learn what truly ticks our wellbeing boxes.

Don't get me wrong, I know it's easier said than done, especially when our bodies are changing, it's bloody difficult! I write this whilst my body has almost zero Estrogen standing slightly crumbled in the middle of the circus that is an NHS post-covid crisis and a national HRT shortage. As

my physical and mental health flags I'm somehow miraculously clinging on waiting for medication, expertise and proper support. I have to remind myself of the badass within! Where there are gaps in the system, I'm moving my focus on what I do have, the things in my control. For starters I have resilience, because I, like you, have overcome everything I have had to face, with the ability to metaphorically put one foot in front of the other...however small those steps may be.

How we fuel or move our bodies, mentally check in, or socially show up, we're all craving that golden key of consistency. When it comes to what we place in the 'box of wellbeing' it feels like we're balancing everything, the habits that form our routine and even the money we spend or save. Yet life often stands firmly in between us and that perfect wellness door, so I'm not going to make you count every step on that thing on your wrist...you can relax, grab a cuppa with a biscuit and read on!

We're all good enough in our imperfect inconsistent human way. So, everything I've added in here is not to make you feel you should be more, or do it all. It's written purely with love, just here if you feel you need to change something up or try something new, spark an idea or move forward on a small goal, that is all. I'd also like to throw a massive caveat in and say I did not do all the things in this book all at once. Some I totally love, they even come easy, and some not so much. In fact, it was and still is a bit of an expedition that I'm trying to balance. Adapting for my ever-changing needs as I go along.

Through any CHANGE there's a lot going on... so just focusing on small 1 improvements is ok.

I too am writing my own rules!

Rule 1   Connect To Your Wellbeing

Our life, energy levels and commitments are fluid, we change as those around us come and go and our environment and circumstances get messed up too. So don't beat yourself up about flitting from one thing to another, there's no room for 'should haves or could haves', you're trying to find what works for you alongside what you've got on. That feeling of giving up or failure is not needed here either...you're exploring! When you can knock that expectation down a few pegs, it really can feel like a bit of an epiphany moment.

Remember your wellbeing is what brings you a sense of quality to your life. To make a shift you can sack off that 100 per cent emoji...just one per cent will do. One per cent is still a step moving forwards. Imagine how far we'd all go and how much better we'd feel if we just kept focusing on that one per cent?

Wellbeing is also our ability to gain that personal quality of life through the physical, mental, emotional, social and spiritual (or woo if you like that term), essences that add to our make-up. As you take a stroll through the sections in this book, you're going to experience all the emotions while you learn to own this time in your life, **because feeling all the feels...that, my friend, is living!**

I'm just going to leave this here...

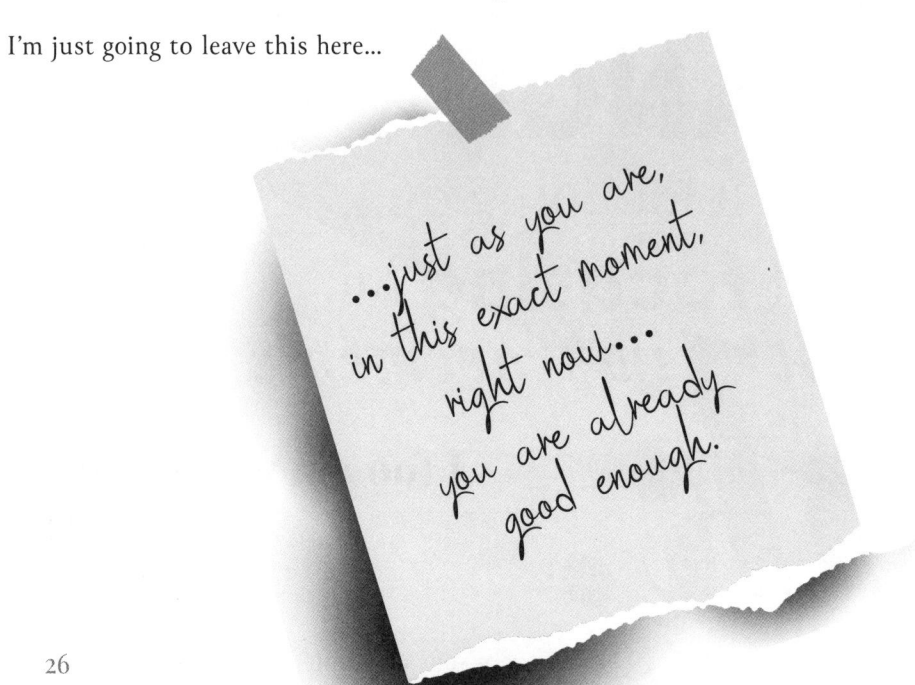

...just as you are, in this exact moment, right now.... you are already good enough.

Rule 1   Connect To Your Wellbeing

RULE 2

UNDERSTANDING THESE
Menopause shenanigans

LET ME EXPLAIN SIMPLY

There are numerous books telling you the ins and outs of all things menopause, with intricate details from a biological and medical point of view. As pre-warned, this is not one of those books.

However...

If this happens to be the first time casting your eyes over anything remotely covering hot sweats, shrivelled vaginas and what might be making you feel like you needed to open the pages, I wouldn't forgive myself if I didn't take a moment to explain what menopause actually means. Put simply:

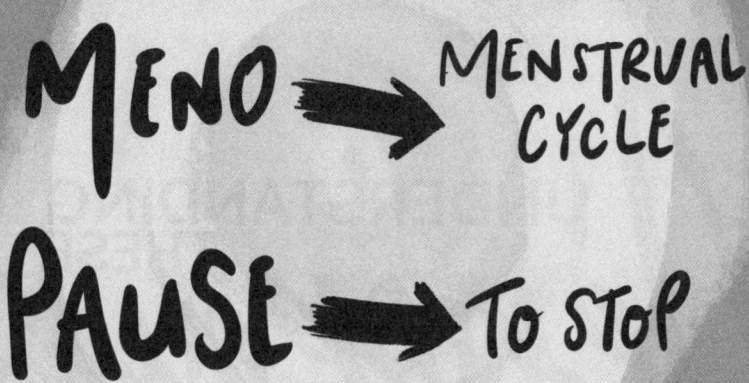

MENO → MENSTRUAL CYCLE

PAUSE → TO STOP

It happens to everyone born with female organs and for most it's a natural (I like to say biological) stage of life.

When a persons' Estrogen hormone levels drop dramatically and they've not had a period for twelve months solid **they have hit menopause**. It's actually only a short amount of time (like a day or something), that you're classed as officially in biological menopause. It's like the tipping point between the before and after.

The 'before' bit is called peri-menopause. It's the time leading up to that biological tipping point. For a lot of people these are the somewhat tricky years as symptoms can last over a decade (I know!), so it's best described as a 'transition', hence why we use the term 'going through it.'

Post menopause is simply the time after periods have stopped altogether, menopause has had its party and you hope you can crack on with the rest of your life. Spoiler alert! For some, symptoms can still be experienced and additional hormone replacement may still be needed. We've just got used to calling all of these stages menopause – I guess for ease.

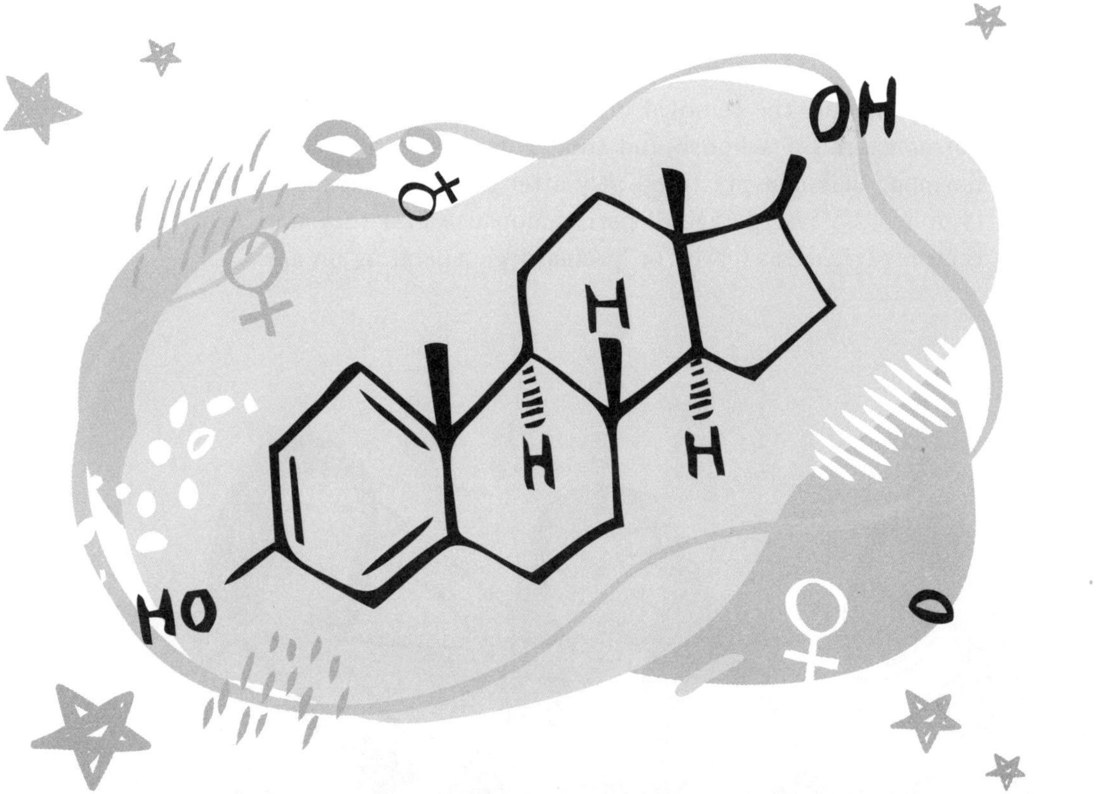

Rule 2   Understand These Menopause Shenanigans

WHAT AGE SHOULD YOU BE MENOPAUSAL?

There is no 'should' about it. The fact is it's different for everyone, depending on circumstance. Although the average age for biological menopause is 45-51, with peri-menopause starting years before, it's already apparent that the conversation needs to come out to play earlier than it currently does. But did you know menopause can hit as early as teens, or as late as sixties, and can come along in many ways? So, let's really crush the taboo!

Early menopause is when symptoms are experienced below the age of 45 and premature menopause is below the age of 40. This can happen for a range of reasons and unfortunately some are still unknown. The ovaries may have stopped working, which is known as **premature ovarian insufficiency or POI**. This could be the result of a trauma through surgery that affects the ovaries long term, some cancer treatments like radiotherapy and chemotherapy, or it may be something genetic or happens with no clear cause, leaving those experiencing it with much more to deal with than just hot flushes.

Surgical menopause is a direct result of surgery. This might be either a full hysterectomy, when the uterus, ovaries and cervix are removed, along with other bits and bobs (depending on type), or an oophorectomy, the removal of the ovaries. There is no slow decline in hormones, it's a 'whoosh and they're gone situation' leaving the person hormone deficient pretty quickly after they leave hospital. If the person is under the average age of peri-menopause (45) they may also refer to their experience as 'early' or 'premature' depending on age.

To complicate matters (because as humans we love to do that), both surgery and treatments that have stopped the ovaries working in an intentional way can also be called **medically induced menopause**. You might also hear the term chemically induced menopause (are you keeping up)? This is where medications are given to, in a sense, switch off the ovaries and can be temporary or permanent; usually to treat cancers, PMDD, help with Fibroids, Endometriosis, Adenomyosis or be used pre-hysterectomy. So, you may hear someone refer to a **medical or chemical menopause**, meaning it's been forced. Again, this can happen much younger than the average age and depending on circumstance, can mean some forms of hormone replacement therapy are simply not at option.

It's good to understand that anyone experiencing menopause much earlier than the average age is likely to be 'hormone deficient' into their fifties and at higher risk of brain, bone and heart problems, as Estrogen is lower if not controlled for many years. Which means they'll be on Hormone Replacement Therapy (HRT), or other medications/supplements if they choose, for possibly decades, sitting in that full blown menopause tipping point for longer than the average person. Welcome to my world!

'We've heard for decades it's a 'women's problem', and yes, sometimes it is problematic and a stage all females will experience, but we mustn't forget **non-binary and transgender menopause** too. Although not everyone in these communities takes hormonal treatments, those taking hormones to feminise will usually take Estrogen and Progesterone with Testosterone blockers. Or to masculinise, Testosterone is taken along with Estrogen blockers. This means they may experience any of the symptoms we see in peri-menopause and again this could be at a much younger age than the average. Societal stigma also factors here, adding another layer of complexity.

All these varying types of experiences that sit outside the average peri-menopausal age bracket can come with a shed load of baggage. This could be fertility grief, physical trauma, cultural stigma, PTS and other mental health issues. The names and lingo are helpful to know, but nothing is more important than just putting the person first before their type of menopause.

Whichever type relates to you the most, I hope that you'll feel connected with at least one of the fabulous people whose stories are weaved throughout these pages. They too have been open and vulnerable in sharing how this new pathway in life has looked and felt for them. Helping *you* unlock a bit of vulnerability to feel ready to fully take on how it shows up for you!

Menopause is not text book, it's more like a biographical story ... and no two are the same.

IT'S JUST HOT FLUSHES AND MOOD SWINGS, RIGHT?

If only! I once heard someone say there are 600 symptoms of menopause. I mean what the...? I nearly spat my coffee out! Do we even have 600 things in our bodies to associate symptoms with? Maybe. So, whilst you're Googling the other 540 odd, I thought I'd give you a list of some of the things to look out for that could be associated with menopause. I say 'could' because these may also be symptoms of something else going on, so always best to keep regular chats in with the doctor if anything concerns you.

Rule 2   Understand These Menopause Shenanigans

I'm sure we'll learn more as the research kicks in, but in the meantime, and for ease, I've left some space for you to make your own notes. You might want to highlight or tick any that immediately resonate with you.

Add any of your additional symptoms here:

PHYSICAL SYMPTOMS

Achey Joints
Allergies Increase or Start
Bad breath
Bleeding Gums
Blood Pressure Changes
Blood Sugar Changes
Bloating
Body Odour
Breast Pain/Tenderness

Breast Size Change
Brittle Nails
Burning Tongue/Mouth
Chills
Cold Sweats
Dizziness (unexplained)
Dry Eyes
Dry Mouth/Tongue
Dull Skin
Electric Shock Feeling

Fatigue
Flooding Periods
Frozen Shoulder
Hair Loss/Thinning
Headaches
Heart Palpitation
Hot Flushes
Incontinence
Insomnia
Irregular Periods
Itchy Skin
Joint Pain
Night Sweats
Pelvic Pain

Restless Legs
Shortness of Breath
Shoulder Pain
Slower Metabolism
Tingling
Tinnitus
Unwanted Hair Growth
UTIs
Vaginal Atrophy
Vaginal Dryness
Vertigo
Weight changes

There are also some other conditions that could be associated such as: heart conditions, Osteoporosis and Fibromyalgia

MENTAL AND EMOTIONAL SYMPTOMS

Anger/Rage
Anxiety
Brain Fog/Memory Loss
Confidence Decreases
Difficulty Concentrating

Irritability
Feeling of Dread
Hormonal Depression
Low Mood
Panic Attacks
Sexual Desire Drops/Increases

Rule 2   Understand These Menopause Shenanigans

So yeah, there's a lot. It doesn't mean you're going to experience them all, if any! Some of you will breeze it, some might only have a few at different stages, whilst for others it might get really tough. The important thing is to **be aware** and not only for yourself. Show your friends, family or partner this list too as they might recognise something in you that you're not seeing yourself. You can tick off any that shout out or re-visit here every so often to check in. Is anything new, changed or gone? The journal section will help you see any patterns so you can summarise at doctors visits.

Additional symptom notes

look how strong you are

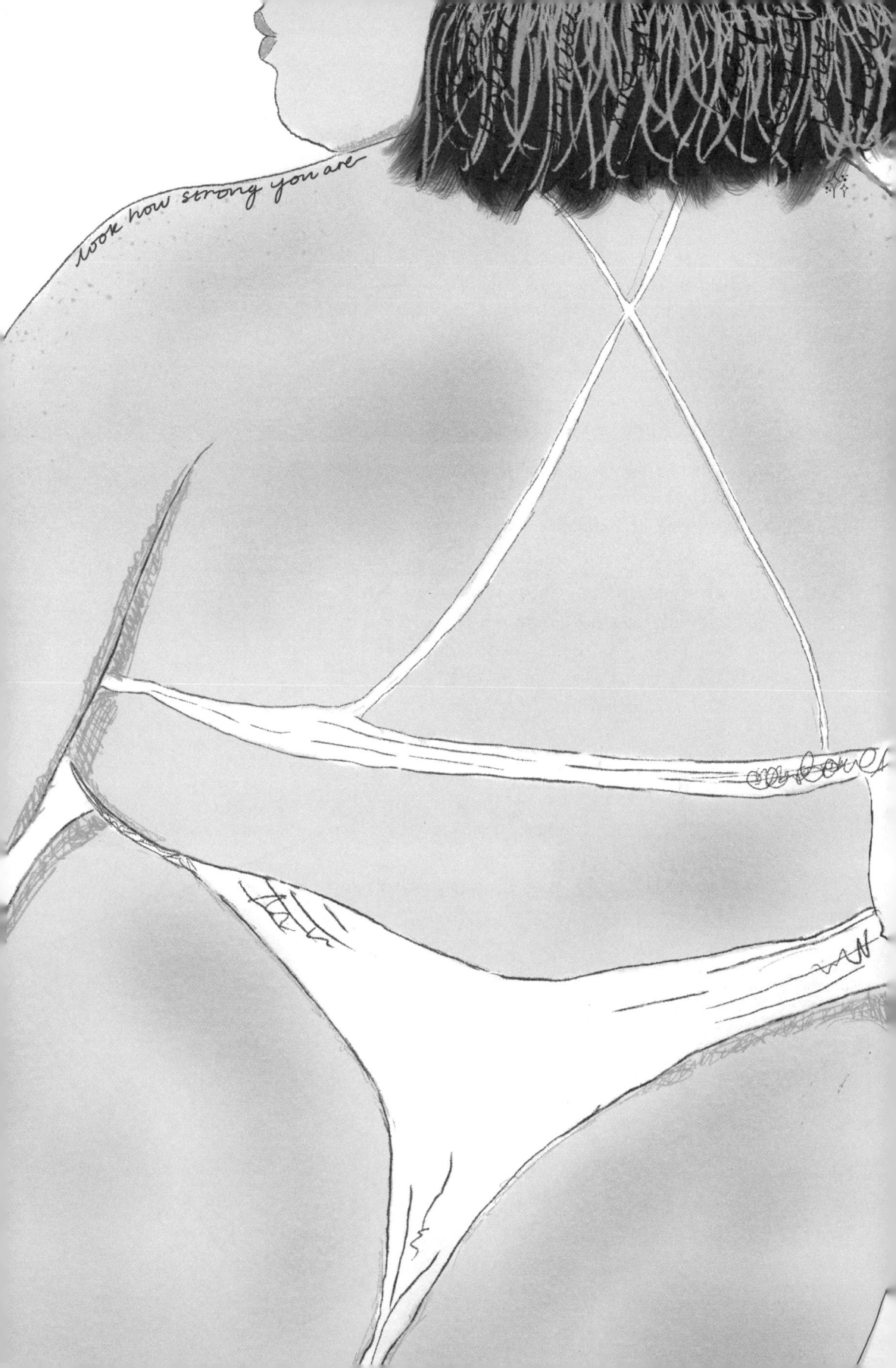

POSITIVITY
PLEASE
Journal Your Mind
gratitude
symptoms
thoughts

RULE 3

JOURNAL, TRACK,
Journal some more

NOTING DOWN YOUR SYMPTOMS AND CHANGES

Whether peri-menopausal, trying a new HRT, recovering from surgery or maybe you just want a general check-in, you've got 12 weeks worth of pages to use as you feel fit.

You might be thinking, 'Three months? Blimey!' But trust me, tracking gives you a fair shot at being able to really see what might be happening over a good period of time. Especially if you're not too sure if you even could be peri-menopausal. This will not only help you, but your doctor too. Journalling over less time is fine, or using it and then coming back later is also cool, do whatever you want…it's your rules!

Important note: If you think there is something really wrong, you're at the end of your tether or muttering 'oh fuck off am I writing down stuff for that long', you absolutely know your body best, so don't hesitate to act on your instinct and seek out professional help.

> "Isn't it funny how DAY BY DAY NOTHING CHANGES, but when we look back, EVERYTHING IS DIFFERENT."
>
> C.S Lewis

Date:

Time to Track

◯ = period / spotting

Day 1 :

◯

Day 2 :

◯

Day 3 :

◯

Day 4 :

◯

Journal / track here!

Day 5 :

Day 6 :

Day 7 :

Notes :

Something I am grateful for...

Date:

Time to Track

◯ = period / spotting

Day 1 :

Day 2 :

Day 3 :

Day 4 :

Day 5 :

Day 6 :

Day 7 :

Journal / track here!

Notes :

Something I am grateful for...

Date:

Time to Track

◯ = period / spotting

Day 1 :

Day 2 :

Day 3 :

Day 4 :

Journal / track here!

Day 5 :

Day 6 :

Day 7 :

Notes :

Something I am grateful for...

Date:

Time to Track

◯ = period / spotting

Day 1 :

Day 2 :

Day 3 :

Day 4 :

Journal / track here!

Day 5 :

Day 6 :

Day 7 :

Notes :

Something I am grateful for...

Date:

Time to Track

◯ = period / spotting

Day 1 :

Day 2 :

Day 3 :

Day 4 :

Journal / track here!

Day 5 :

Day 6 :

Day 7 :

Notes :

Something I am grateful for...

Date:

Time to Track

◯ = period / spotting

Day 1 :

Day 2 :

Day 3 :

Day 4 :

Day 5 :

Day 6 :

Day 7 :

Journal / track here!

Something I am grateful for...

Notes :

Date:

Time to Track

○ = period / spotting

Day 1 :

Day 2 :

Day 3 :

Day 4 :

Journal / track here!

Day 5 :

Day 6 :

Day 7 :

Notes :

Something I am grateful for...

Date:

Time to Track

◯ = period / spotting

Day 1 :

Day 2 :

Day 3 :

Day 4 :

Day 5 :

Day 6 :

Day 7 :

Journal / track here!

Notes :

Something I am grateful for...

Date:

Time to Track

◯ = period / spotting

Day 1 :

Day 2 :

Day 3 :

Day 4 :

Journal / track here!

Day 5 :

Day 6 :

Day 7 :

Notes :

Something I am grateful for...

61

Date:

Time to Track

◯ = period / spotting

Day 1 :

Day 2 :

Day 3 :

Day 4 :

Journal / track here!

Day 5 :

Day 6 :

Day 7 :

Something I am grateful for...

Notes :

Date:

Time to Track

◯ = period / spotting

Day 1 :

Day 2 :

Day 3 :

Day 4 :

Day 5 :

Day 6 :

Day 7 :

Journal / track here!

Notes :

Something I am grateful for...

Date:

Time to Track

◯ = period / spotting

Day 1 :

Day 2 :

Day 3 :

Day 4 :

Day 5 :

Day 6 :

Day 7 :

Journal / track here!

Notes :

Something I am grateful for...

67

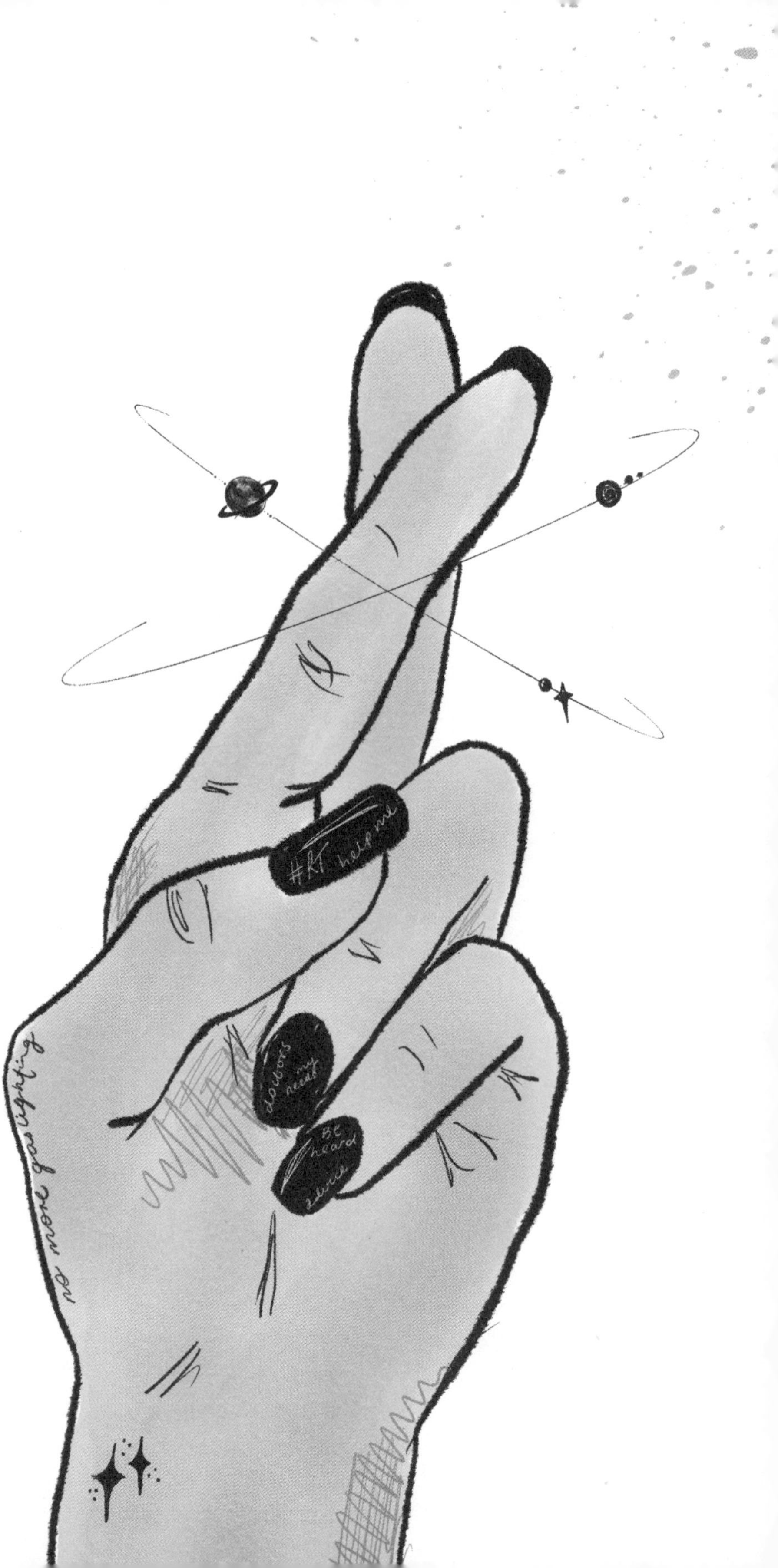
#RT help me
doctors
my needs
Be heard
no more gaslighting

RULE 4

GET THE *medical stuff* IN ORDER

THE DOCTOR WILL SEE YOU NOW...TIME TO BE EMPOWERED

Being prepped for your time with medical professionals, whether a GP, consultant or in post-surgery appointments is – and I cannot stress this enough – like having a freakin' superpower. It's easy to step through that door with it all in your head only to freeze in the moment as they ask, 'so what's been happening?' or fire their questions, views and possibly 'fob offs' your way, all whilst that ticking clock on the wall accompanies your appointment like the music on that TV show 'Countdown'!

I've had to fight for myself medically for a long time, through my Endometriosis diagnosis, high risk pregnancies, premature births and even how I demanded to be re-sown up after a hash job on my beautiful vulva after childbirth. However, when I hit the big M it somehow wasn't that easy for me to step up – maybe I was just exhausted!

Trusting way too much in poor or limited information, little prior knowledge of surgical menopause had me thrown in the deep end after surgery and it seemed to pass me by just how hormonally deficient I'd be and what that even meant. I didn't ask the questions and was **underprepared for what I'd need**. I wasn't curious enough and didn't start to piece things together until I was sat in a stuffy hospital room trying to work through the fuzz of depression and unpicking the scabs of the wounds I was trying to heal.

This was way too late!

You can know with certainty that you'll advocate for yourself like a pro from now on. Until the time comes when we can be sure we'll always be listened to and supported, with a holistic and empathetic viewpoint... aaaah, now wouldn't that be amazing?

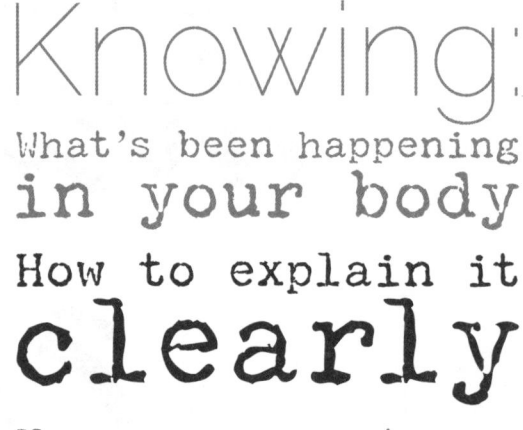

Knowing:
What's been happening in your body
How to explain it clearly
How you expect any appointments to go
...is how you take ownership.

Along with consistently tracking symptoms over clear timeframes, being well prepped and setting your own agenda is going to give you power! So, guess what? I've included some things that might just help.

> **Note!** I can't possibly include every eventuality or the many parts of the journey you are on, so forgive me. But here's your space to get organised, have some back up knowledge and make notes so you can kick some advocating arse!

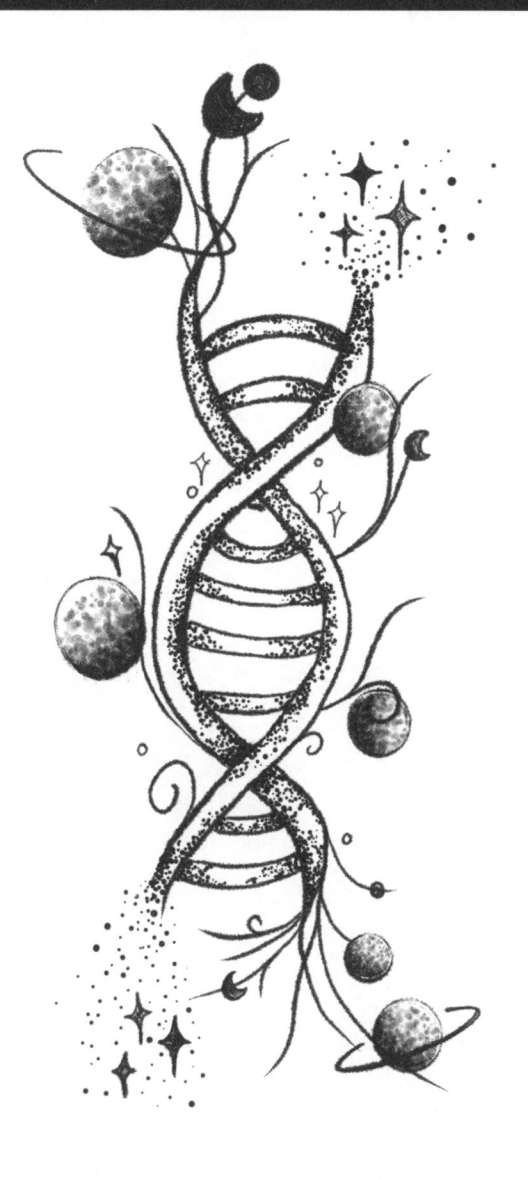

WHAT YOUR DOCTOR MIGHT ASK

It's useful to have an idea of what you might be asked *before* your appointment as it might help you process, give some prior thought to answers, or even trigger you in some way so you're not caught off guard. What is asked may differ depending on who you're seeing, and if there's anything you *really* want to raise, offer the information up! Doctors see a lot of people so how can you make it easier for them too? You'll get more out of the appointment and having the answers with you saves heaps of time, alleviating those brain fog moments, and it'll be easier to go through emotionally because you'll have prepped like a pro!

Rule 4   Get The Medical Stuff In Order

My Menopause, My Journal, My Rules!

Info To Offer The Doctor

Height:

Weight:

Smoker/drugs use:

Alcohol intake:

Regular medications inc. HRT:

Any relevant medical conditions:

Any operations/treatments?

Do you have a womb/ovaries?

Any previous pregnancies?

72

Doctors Notes

Could you be pregnant?

Are you on contraception?

When was your last period?

If relevant – when are you due a smear test?

If relevant – when are you due for a mammogram?

Do you have any serious bleeding?

Are you experiencing vaginal dryness?

What symptoms are you most worried about?

Do you have particular questions or concerns about HRT?

Rule 4   Get The Medical Stuff In Order

TO HRT OR NOT TO HRT

Hormone Replacement Therapy...what can sometimes seem like the gold at the end of the rainbow, has certainly been controversial chatter for decades for many differing reasons. My knowledge spans as far as tablet, patch, gel, pessary, implant and chocolate, all things that I have tried. I couldn't reel off all the differing names, dosages and who makes them, but I do know it's been and still is a ride in finding what works! I've lathered myself up with high dosages of gels many a time, walking around looking like I'm some sort of half-naked wet weirdo shouting 'don't touch me!' to any adult or child that comes within a metre, all to learn I don't actually absorb the stuff that well! Because of the complexity of HRT, there are far more sensible, medically-trained people to seek out, who should tailor to your personal needs. So, we're keeping it light touch – sorry not sorry – I have my reasons for not bringing a menopause doctor into the folds of this section...read on and I'll explain.

However, it's helpful to give a very brief overview of the differing forms HRT comes in, before moving on:

- **Estrogen** – there is oh so much to this female hormone and it's probably the one we hear about the most. In a nutshell, it helps keep our brains, hearts and really our whole selves healthy.

- **Progesterone** – taken to compliment Estrogen it helps with various symptoms, but sleep is a big one and it can regulate peri-menopausal bleeds. It's also given post-hysterectomy to those who have had Endometriosis.

- **Testosterone** – This little kicker gives confidence, get up and go and can help increase the want for sexy time!

How your body gets the stuff can vary between oral daily tablets, patches big and small (that you change every few days), gels, sprays, vaginal pessaries and even implants. There are Bio-identical and Bio-genetic, some sit within the healthcare system and some outside. Some you'll get because you live in a certain part of the world, some you won't because it's a bit of a lottery. Your doctor might offer you all the above to choose, or they may advise you take something specific. One could tell you it's going to change your life, whilst another refuses to prescribe it all. And then there's the times you get prescribed anti-depressants instead! So, you can see why I've not got my white coat on and filled the pages here. There are also amazing menopause specialists that have already shared knowledge and their thoughts in places just waiting for you to watch, listen or read, so no need to duplicate and complicate, but remember it's still not as simple as what options are stated in a book.

You need to have your game face on and the want to understand, persevere and acknowledge that it's going to be a journey, maybe a bit of a fight, but let me tell you...you are so worth it!

I don't want to piss on anyone's fireworks here, but it's important to remember: yes, check out websites/socials, read some great books, chat to coaches, or listen to podcasts and of course find out what Sandra down the road is on because she's loving life in 'the change'. Because this will all help you become informed, see the possibilities and get you ready with some questions. However, some of this is generic, not gospel and sometimes not appropriate.

Please use the information you're soaking up as an aid to speak to a doctor you trust, who's got an interest in menopause or is a specific menopause consultant. Discuss what HRT means for you, how you want to explore this and work through the myths, pros and cons together. I guess what I'm saying is 'use your loaf!' Think about where you spend your money, and who you're seeking information from. You'd be surprised how many people ask me for medical advice, simply because I can dance like a twat on social media and share my experience. But my experience is not yours. We all have different requirements, budgets and circumstances, so if you feel lost in the noise of it all, centre yourself back to *your* needs, how *you* want to *feel* and remember that HRT is only part of the puzzle.

> **Important note!**
> These are the big three that keep us functioning. So understand which ones you're lacking in so you know what you need to demand for, filling any gaps. There's much more to them in terms of what their functions are, how they interact with other things in our bodies, such as Histamine for example, so if you like to know the depths of detail, set some research time aside.

Now...your ears may have pricked up when reading through the different ways to get HRT into your system, depending on your lifestyle, or maybe you're on something now and it's not working for you. Make the time to explore. I know I'm not handing it to you on a plate, but I want you to

Rule 4   Get The Medical Stuff In Order

seek out the relevant and up to date information, at the time that you're reading this. As I said, it might be a bit of a climb to what works for you, and it'll take some tweaking (believe me I'm still tweaking!). What I can give you is some space to write anything HRT related that you find helpful or want to raise with the GP.

One important thing I will share though is what a menopause doctor said to me, which I think is really important to remember:

If HRT is working effectively, you shouldn't be experiencing any symptoms.

I hear way too often from people that they are on HRT and yet their symptoms are off the scale and we just get on with it. This should not be the case and is where we should be tweaking things.

My HRT Notes:

Rule 4 Get The Medical Stuff In Order

My Menopause, My Journal, My Rules!

BE APPOINTMENT READY!

Use this next section for multiple appointments (GP/gynaecologist/consultant/menopause doctor) if needed. Take this book with you so you have everything you need in one place and lead with your agenda on how you want the conversation to go. You can refer to the HRT section too. For extra support you could:

- Print out the free 'NICE' guidelines online to offer to the GP. These show what they should be following for your age range, and they might not have seen them yet.

- Take a mate with you who can speak up for you if you feel you can't at this time.

NOTES FROM THE APPOINTMENT

To save you feeling anxious that you'll forget what's been said, I've also added space to jot down what's been discussed. If you leave this book at home use your phone: voice record or text/type notes and write up later. You are allowed to take notes... it's *your* health appointment!

Rule 4   Get The Medical Stuff In Order

My Menopause, My Journal, My Rules!

Appointment Prep

Date of appointment:

I'm seeing/contact details:

Today I want to talk about:

Time-frame symptoms tracked:

My physical symptoms:

My mental/emotional symptoms:

The outcome I want:

My questions:

What my appointment covered:

Next steps:

Additional notes:

Appointment Notes

Rule 4 Get The Medical Stuff In Order

My Menopause, My Journal, My Rules!

Appointment Prep

Date of appointment:

I'm seeing/contact details:

Today I want to talk about:

Time-frame symptoms tracked:

My physical symptoms:

My mental/emotional symptoms:

The outcome I want:

My questions:

What my appointment covered:

Next steps:

Additional notes:

Appointment Notes

Rule 4 Get The Medical Stuff In Order

Appointment Prep

Date of appointment:

I'm seeing/contact details:

Today I want to talk about:

Time-frame symptoms tracked:

My physical symptoms:

My mental/emotional symptoms:

The outcome I want:

My questions:

What my appointment covered:

Next steps:

Additional notes:

Appointment Notes

Rule 4 — Get The Medical Stuff In Order

My Menopause, My Journal, My Rules!

Appointment Prep

Date of appointment:

I'm seeing/contact details:

Today I want to talk about:

Time-frame symptoms tracked:

My physical symptoms:

My mental/emotional symptoms:

The outcome I want:

My questions:

What my appointment covered:

Next steps:

Additional notes:

Appointment Notes

Rule 4   Get The Medical Stuff In Order

WHAT ABOUT THE ALTERNATIVES?

For some of you, HRT just isn't an option. This might be because you've been advised, or for personal reasons. There are various other medications such as forms of anti-depressants (they can help flushes) along with supplements you can try to help ease symptoms. Later we start to delve further beyond tinctures, so you can build your personal prescription with balance in a way that speaks to your whole self. For now, let's talk supplements. Because I don't absorb Estrogen all that well – meaning I had long periods with almost zero in my body – I decided to do some research and chat to various people who can't take HRT, to see the alternatives. Before I entered into this trial-and-error world I was bit of an inconsistent multi-vitamin gal, but I'm now starting to learn what is working for me. Like HRT, there are a lot of choices: what to take, which brand, and marketing comes into play here too. Do some digging and go with what you can afford at the time. The rubbish thing is, when HRT isn't an option it's down to your hand in your own pocket...so again, have your wits about you!

Here's some things I've tried with my honest reviews :

- **CBD:** I like the oil capsules, also comes in oil or gummies. Naturally calming, it reduces cortisol (the stress hormone) helping with joint pain and sleep. It took the edge of my depression and anxiety and I could change my dose easily when needed. I don't get side effects, but it's not the cheapest, although it's becoming much more available.

- **5HTP:** Helps with depression, reduces migraines and helps sleep. Must not be taken with CBD but is a cheaper alternative.

- **EVENING PRIMROSE OIL:** Helps with hot flushes. Some like this a lot. I didn't see the benefit.

- **ASHWAGANDHA:** Good for muscle strength, sharpens focus and memory and could help libido. Can also help sleep. This gave me some trippy dreams when I started, which wore off in a few days.

- **BLACK MACCA:** Boosts energy, libido, sharpens mind and helps metabolism. Take in the morning!

- **MAGNESIUM CITRATE:** added to drinking water this apparently helps nights sweats. Although I didn't feel the benefit, I love the stuff as a good all rounder.

- **VITAMIN D:** Improves bone pain and helps you feel less lethargic. If you can't get some natural rays, sup it up. You might even want to ask for a blood test as it's common for this to drop in Menopause.

- **B VITAMINS:** B2 for thinning hair and skin, B3 helps anxiety and menstrual headaches, B6 for bloating and moods, B9 for brain fog and B12 helps low, depressive moods and increases energy, fighting fatigue. I opt for a banging pea protein powder that doubles up as a multivitamin including all the B vitamins I need and bonus extras. This tastes good and is easier on the pennies.

- **MAGNESIUM:** Tablets, baths salts, oil or sprays…go for it! Helps bloods sugar levels, PMDD, depression, is anti-inflammatory and gives a boost when you're trying to move your body.

- **COLLAGEN:** My budget doesn't stretch to liquid, so I take a capsule. Can be a good marine oil or vegan. Helps with joints, strengthens hair against thinning and improves skin, helping to replace where our Estrogen lacks. The first thing I noticed was my joints ached less and my lashes were insane! I do think I've got a bit of a glow back. I'm yet to see the improvements in hair thinning, but it feels in better condition.

- **BLACK COHOSH:** Helps with hot flushes, night sweats, irritability and even vaginal dryness. Loads of people swear by this, but I didn't feel the benefits and they say you shouldn't take for more than a year.

- **STARFLOWER OIL:** Improves joint pain, improves hormonal skin and this really helped with the pain I got in my breasts, it's reasonably priced too.

> **Important note:**
> Always ask your doctor before taking anything as some supplements, like food, can cause uproar in your body if you have certain conditions such as diabetes or heart conditions.

There are so many more and I think the moral is to give whatever your budget allows a go. Monitor for three weeks at least and see how you feel. Everyone is different, but essentially nothing is going to replace Estrogen fully, we can only do what we can all round to improve how we feel.

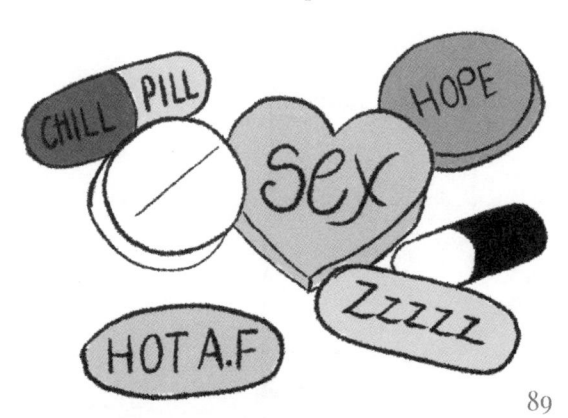

My Menopause, My Journal, My Rules!

Here is space for you to make any notes of any supplements you're currently finding out about. Use the journal section too if it helps track.

My supplement notes:

TAKE WITH A PINCH OF OPTIMISM, SOME TRIAL AND ERROR, WITH A DOSE OF PATIENCE!

My supplement notes:

TAKE WITH A PINCH OF OPTIMISM, SOME TRIAL AND ERROR, WITH A DOSE OF PATIENCE!

'MEDICAL GASLIGHTING' – IT'S NOT OKAY

Most people in the healthcare profession are blooming amazing, wanting to help you as best they can, and no-one is really out to do a bad job. It's often systems, strategy and money that create the mountains *we* and *they* have to climb. However, 'medical gaslighting' unfortunately happens and I've experienced this on numerous occasions. 'It's just heavy periods, totally normal when you're young.' Nope, Endometriosis. Or I've been made to feel like my pain wasn't as bad as it was. I can tell you, when you've had twelve ruptured ovarian cysts, you know that pain is not a good sign! One not so friendly midwife once spat, 'I think you're being a little dramatic about your worries.'

Pregnant with my son and following a miscarriage I was explaining to her the trauma of my daughter's birth at twenty-five weeks. I was twenty-three at that time, with the entire cast of 'Casualty' in the room, haemorrhaging as the doctor had both hands in my vagina saying, 'We won't resuscitate if the baby isn't breathing on their own,' and I was 300 miles away from my house! 'So don't tell me I'm being fucking dramatic to worry about this upcoming labour!' She was a lot more empathetic after that download!

Despite this, please **don't feel fearful of talking to anyone,** the good far outweigh the bad. However, by understanding this *could* happen, you can be on the right side of it if it does. You might have a 'ah hang on a minute' moment whilst they chat, where you recognise something is amiss. Then you can think about what your next move is.

For now let me explain what medical gaslighting feels like:

Minimising
This is where your symptoms are dismissed. They could be debilitating but you are made to feel that they're trivial or not as bad as they are.

Downplaying
This is when you may be made to feel like you're making it up, or is disregarded as something else.

Blaming
This is where ailments are blamed on something else unrelated. The conversation could shift to question your trustworthiness: 'I think you're overreacting or being a bit sensitive', or question your memory of the event asking 'are you sure?' Psychological factors or deliberate use of negative stereotypes around your gender, race, age or ethnicity could be brought in.

Refusing
Your concerns are simply not listened to; you don't feel heard or supported. There is complete denial as to what you're going through completely.

If something is said that doesn't feel right, or your gut is having a niggle, go with your instinct and call it out there and then, if you're feeling up to it. If that gives you the jeebies, simply walk away, reflect on the conversation and go up the line with a well written email. Press send and then book an appointment to see someone else. If they've done it to you, they'll have done it before and most likely do it to others. It's not an acceptable practice of any decent healthcare professional, **end of!**

INTERVAL OF EVENTS

As I write this medical section, I'm literally having to advocate for my own health, trying everything to keep myself level and not lose my shit again. I'm up against the joys of an over stretched under (menopause) educated GP surgery and the mafia of receptionists, from pleasant Anna who's so helpful, to Gloria who is quite frankly a bit of a cunt!

After the news that a new menopause clinic was now attached to my surgery had me dancing around the kitchen, I was swiftly on a phone consultation with a Meno doctor who was located over an hour away from my GP. I finally felt heard; it was marvellous. She quickly confirmed that I don't absorb Estrogen despite the eight gel pumps I'd been lathering myself up with for the best part of two years. She also prescribed Progesterone – apparently this was a must due to my Endometriosis. She couldn't quite believe I hadn't been given this after surgery four years ago; bloody brilliant! She requested for some bloods, then suggested I'd do well with the Estrogen implant. How easy was that? Oh, how fucking wrong could I be?

What followed has been quite a shit show of back and forth chasing the surgery daily for lost blood results, misinformed communication, wrong prescription orders and a huge lack of empathy. My Estrogen level is thirty-seven...I mean I'm practically dead on the Estrogen scale for someone in surgical menopause!

'I'm not sure how you're functioning,' the GP almost sings as she checks my palpitating tight chest with an ECG.

'I'm fucking not,' I think to myself, both my physical and mental symptoms playing a cruel game with me, whilst I comprehend that I've still been managing to do all the things on just ten per cent of a tank!

I'm actually a hero.

No-one knows your body more than YOU know your body... period.

keep going
you're so
worth it!

Rule 4 Get The Medical Stuff In Order

there is so much energy... rose & bone

RULE 5

BE WELL PREPPED FOR THE *'No-Ovary Club'*

SURGERIES THAT IMPACT

Hysterectomy – A surgical procedure to remove the womb (uterus), which is done by either laparoscopic key-hole, vaginally or abdominally.

There are different types of hysterectomy ranging from just removing your uterus to taking everything including ovaries, fallopian tubes, cervix and surrounding tissues. If the ovaries are removed, periods stop, and surgical menopause begins immediately, if you aren't menopausal already. If the ovaries are staying put although you won't be in surgical menopause you may enter an earlier than usual peri-menopause due to blood supply being disrupted. Depending on age this could be classed as POI.

Main reasons a hysterectomy is needed:

- ✓ Dangerously heavy periods
- ✓ Fibroids
- ✓ Endometriosis
- ✓ Adenomyosis
- ✓ Prolapse
- ✓ Cancer of the womb, ovaries or cervix
- ✓ PMDD - Pre-Menstrual Dysphoric Disorder

Oophorectomy – A surgical procedure to remove one or both ovaries, usually by laparoscopy, vaginally or abdominal incision.

This can also include the fallopian tubes and the removal of both ovaries will again cause surgical menopause immediately. If both ovaries and fallopian tubes are removed you won't be able to get pregnant naturally, however if the uterus is left you may be able to carry using IVF. There may be ways you can preserve fertility before the procedure such as freezing eggs, so it's good to have this conversation early on if it feels right for you.

Main Reasons a oophorectomy is needed:

- ✓ Ovarian cancer
- ✓ Endometriosis
- ✓ Ovarian cysts

✓ Preventative surgery for those carrying the BRCA gene
✓ Pelvic inflammatory disease (PID)
✓ Ovarian torsion affecting the blood supply and causing pain
✓ Fallopian tube issues such as: twisting or the result on a ectopic pregnancy

Whatever the procedure it's important to chat through the lingo with your consultant and understand all the risks, options and impact on your life after.

TEQUILA SHOTS, DVT SOCKS AND HOT DOCS
HOW IT WAS FOR ME

Sitting with my consultant, we chatted through what would happen during the surgery, what type of hysterectomy I was having and he reiterated that kids would no longer be an option. Although I'd had my two and my uterus was a mess, I still felt an extreme ache inside that having no more was suddenly out of my hands, with no gradual natural end to this era. What if years later I changed my mind? He informed me what, medically, would need to be done beforehand. I say 'medically' because I was swiftly put on Zoladex, a monthly implant I'd need for six months leading up to the operation. My Endometriosis and Adenomyosis were in so many places; 'this will hopefully help clean things up, reducing the mess and complications of the surgery', he reassured.

I visited the nurse every month who kindly shot in this little pellet next to my belly button, checked my blood pressure and asked how I was feeling. She'd commented on how young I was and she told me this drug was used to treat prostate cancer, mentioning I may even lose my hair.

Although my red mane was kind of my signature, this side effect didn't compare to the reality of possibly coming out the other side with a colonoscopy bag – the Endometriosis was on my bowel too.

'The Zoladex might feel like a mini-menopause, you know a few hot flushes,' she muttered. 'Hot flushes? Okay,' I thought. 'I mean that's all the menopause is, right?' Not a mini-menopause at all, I now know this was chemically induced menopause, a very different thing indeed!

Closer to the op the consultant explained about my physical recovery and the need for rest: 'No hoovering, driving or lifting anything more than a kettle, okay?' he said adamantly. I would need between six to ten weeks off work, oh, and he flippantly mentioned how I'd need to take HRT for the next couple of decades...that was kind of my lot! I remember thinking, 'Wow, it's really important for me not to lift more than a kettle...who the hell is going to do all the housework?'

As I got closer to the hysterectomy, I'd got more comfortable with the thought of no more kids. I realised I was grieving for something that was hugely unlikely to happen, let alone be safe. Instead, I focused on who and what I had around me. My priority was to be a healthy Mum to the kids I had, not think about an imaginary future fantasy I didn't even know if I truly wanted!

However my mind was all over the show when it came to what was about to happen, sending my overthinking off the scale; what if it doesn't work? What if they find cancer or my bowel is damaged and I have to shit through a bag? What if they slice through my spine and I'm paralysed? OMG maybe removing my cervix means I'll never orgasm again? Oh god, what if I die on the table (to be fair this haunted me at every op I'd had)? How will my husband raise the kids on his own? Because, let's be honest, I'm not one of those 'I just want you to re-marry and be happy' types! And what if there's some proper fit doctor present who is going to see me – literally – in all my glory? FUCK!

I stressed over everything, A LOT. To the point where the divorce statistics were about to go up. I questioned how everyone would cope, be places, tidy, cook, organise and do ALL the things whilst I was recovering. This makes me chuckle now because, thank goodness, they learnt quickly, as quite honestly I'm a bit pants at organising a shopping list nowadays! I also went out on a mahoosive piss up two nights before my surgery, you know in case I 'never came back!' These are words I vaguely remember slurring to various friends as I downed Tequila! Drinking habits aside, I did manage to squeeze in quality time with the family and even a run on the morning before we arrived at the hospital…I know get me! But the overthinking and worrying about everyone else took president to the proper planning, getting mindful tools in place and organisation of my own body and mind.

Before I knew it, what felt like an endless wait and a million repetitive questions was over and I was fired up for life to come, walking in my new slippers and fetching DVT socks down to theatre as my arse peeked out the back of my gown. Entering the little room adjacent to where the chopstick mayhem would commence, I could see them prepping. 'Fuck, this is it!' danced in my head as I got up onto the table ready for the nap of all naps. Then he walked in…piercing eyes, his October skin holding the colour of summer, biceps slightly bulging under the green scrubs… he was the Mr Grey of anaesthetists. 'Double Fuck…' I whispered as his kind voice asked me to lie down. He held my hand (probably more professionally than I'd like to recall) as he sent me off with his wonder drug. Well, if a girl's gonna die on the table, at least she goes out to that, I thought. **Zzzzzzz!**

Back in the room, I dozed on and off as I tried to focus on the words from my consultant (why do they always come when you're out of it?). 'I'm pleased to say the Zoladex did the job, your hysterectomy was a success, very clean sweep, no nasties,' were his words as I lay there rather hazy. My years of pain gone, like someone had flicked a switch whilst I slept. I could feel my legs properly, the nice neat wounds over my previous scars slightly throbbed and, hurrah, my bowel was fully intact. Thanks universe!

After four days (I proper milked it) and with the get well cards collected, I grabbed the mini balloon the kids had placed in one of those cardboard things you stick a penis in to wee and waved farewell to the view outside, which had been my aim to walk towards. It was time to go home. I left hospital hoping to be a stone lighter from my lack of womb (I wasn't) and rocking my baggy soft trousers I hobbled out with nothing more than a leaflet on how to poop, a box of HRT tablets and the prospect that my husband might cook for me for the first time in fifteen years!

As far as we could tell I was Endo free and the high risk of cancer (of at least those bits) had rightfully done one with the rest of the organs in the pan. And once this girl was healed, she was going to have the best sex of her pain free life, with the husband of course, I never got the anaesthetist's number! I was grateful, excited, tired and sore…but finally hopeful again.

COMMUNICATION AND CURIOSITY IS UNDERRATED

The thing is there were so many gaps in what I was told about the whole shindig, it was like I got the card through the door for the delivery but never quite received the full package. Equally, I didn't ask. Maybe I was too trusting, a little naive or tired of having to advocate and tired of all the operations that I'd had before. There was so much I didn't know and ways I could have prepared better, with a complete lack of connection between what was going to happen physically and what might come along mentally and socially after an operation like this.

Looking back there are some things I could have done differently. But my learns are your gains so this little bit is here as your 'Zoladex', you know, to help clean up the mess of the unknown and tidy up some stuff before and after your surgery. Here's some things I did and some I wish I had!

Leading up to the big day:

```
Share how you feel. Whether loved ones or a
coach or therapist, knowing what this all
means to you and chatting it over beforehand
helps you come to terms with what's happening.
All your feelings are valid.
```

```
If you have little people or teens in your
life, tell them what's going on. Explain (age
appropriately) what will happen physically and
mentally. Reassure them you'll be safe and ask
them what they can do to help you...then fill in
the gaps. Answer their questions honestly.
```

```
Be a little more mindful over what
you eat and drink. Specifically,
alcohol and the sugary stuff. Look
at some pre-op food plans to help
cleanse. Increase your protein.
```

```
Exercise as normal.
```

```
Start supplements that might
help inflammation and any
menopausal symptoms to come
(check with the doctor first).
```

Use your medical sections in here with your consultant. Staple in letters. You may want to ask extra questions about the anaesthetic, risk of prolapse, exercises after and whether you're having keyhole or incision. The recovery may be different.

Research to understand the lingo for your type of hysterectomy. Don't shy away from the risks or things to look out for after so you're empowered to speak up should anything not feel right. Jot it down in this section, it might prompt questions later.

Think about how long your stay is. Use the planner section to write what you want to take, who is doing what and anything you feel you need to get in order!

Get some good stress reducing practises in, check out rule 8 in here or continue what you usually do to help.

Start a good pelvic floor routine. Rule 7 in here is a good starter.

If social media is your thing, follow accounts you relate to. Real people's stories are a great tool alongside the medical guidance.

Research surgical menopause. I know you're here, but I only scratch the surface!

Buy some comfy clothes a couple of sizes up. You won't want to faff with buttons, zips or anything that isn't stretchy for 'swelly belly' or irritate any incisions.

Body pillows are great for comfy sleeping and feeling generally supported. Especially when you need to cough or sneeze and it feels like the world might fall out. Fear not, that feeling will soon pass!

Prep your main rest area at home. Get everything ready to go within reach and at a height where you won't need to over stretch or bend down.

Rally up the troops! Who's going to help you? Talk to family, friends or neighbours. Let them know what's to come - there's no shame in telling them what will help.

Get some easy dinners prepped in the freezer, to save on Deliveroo becoming your best mate and rinsing your bank balance!

Rule 5   Be Well Prepped For 'The No Ovary Club'

THINGS TO DO BEFORE SURGERY

Things I need to arrange:

The hospital bag:

Medications and Supplements I take:

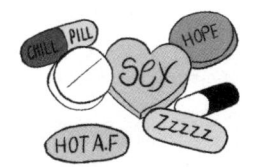

Questions for the big day:

Rule 5　Be Well Prepped For 'The No Ovary Club'

In your own way you gave me strength,
You were the energetic portal between
all that is and all that will be,
Your divine power walked with me,
We have lived all we have together...
and for that I am grateful to you.

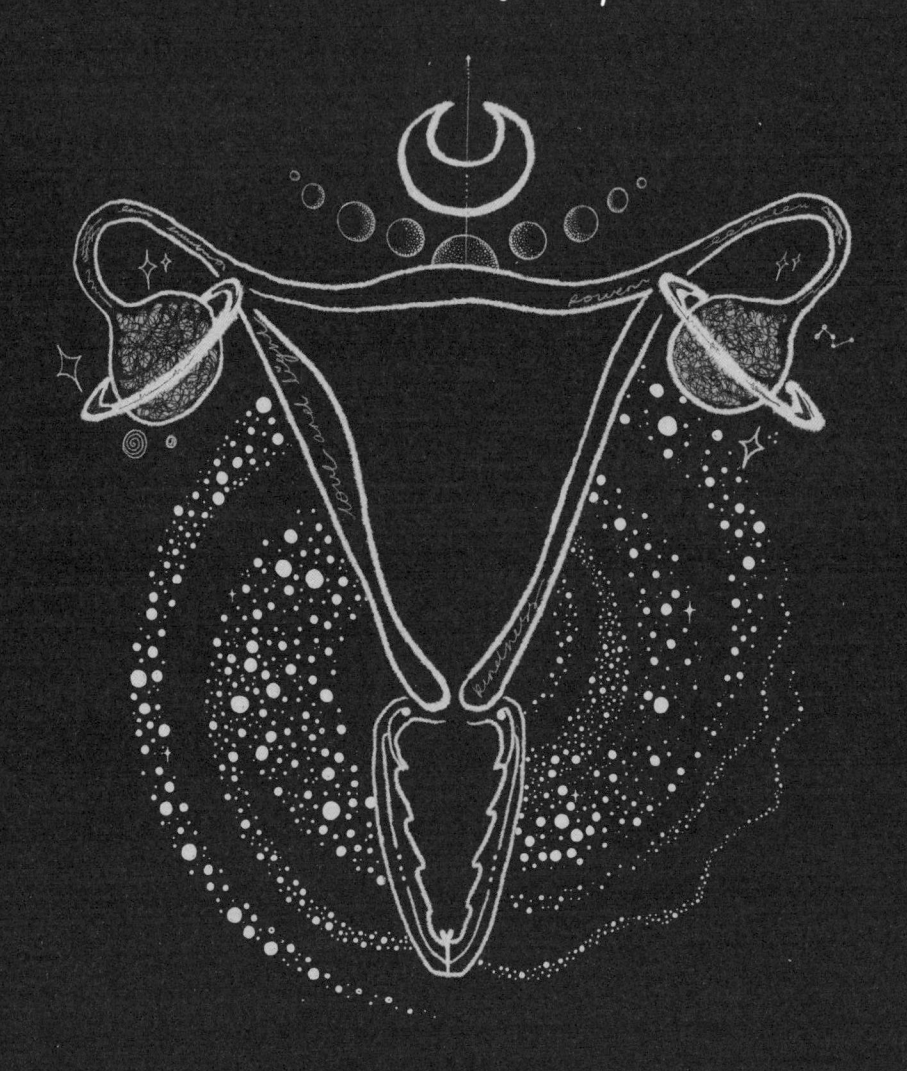

PART ON GOOD TERMS

I want you to take a moment before you have your operation to be with the parts that are being removed. Bear with me. **Our body really can hold trauma** so a few days before you go in, take time to sit quietly in a space and focus on the parts that you'll be saying goodbye to. Let the feelings arise and any emotions come, sit with them for a while and then allow it all to move through you. Whatever you feel try to acknowledge it, however hard, I get it. This might feel weird or tough, you could be feeling deep grief or simply thinking get this out of me. It might be you feel let down or even angry at what's inside...this is all valid so try to connect.

Because these organs have been with you since the beginning, and although the biological pieces within are bidding farewell, the energy held in your core is supercharged. It is not the fault of your uterus/ovaries/cervix, or whatever names resonate, that you're embarking on this surgery and new path...it is beyond blame. They all did their best to serve you and in your own way you'll have grown through its power and will remain to grow fierce, into a new era with an awakened energy shift. Try to sit in that thought. Where there is loss there is always love, be kind to your body and try to send this part of you some thanks as it passes on. This is something I wish I'd done.

THE AFTER (OP) PARTY

- Drink the prune juice, it'll help you go for that first poo.

- It's not a heart attack, it's wind. If you're going key hole you might get an awful pain in your shoulder. You'll be like 'what the hell is that?' Mention it to the nurse, but I'm pretty sure they'll say you just need a good fart!

- They'll quickly encourage you out of bed, it'll feel scary and weird but it gets things moving. Use the window or a picture to aim for, stop and just take it in. You took the first steps - go you!

- Tuck your body pillow or a folded blanket between you and the seatbelt for that journey home and any you might take in the first few days.

- Let stuff go. No-one is you, so others won't do all the things in the way you like to do them! The novelty of helping might wear off for the other members of the household, try not to lose it with them…if you feel like murder is possible, immediately go to the 'scream on a page' in here.

- REST…small walks…REST again! Don't be a dick (like me) and think after a week you'll decide, 'I know…I'll just hoover the stairs.' Epic fail!

- Listen to your body, it will feel tired for maybe longer than you imagine. Those symptoms might kick off and emotions may ride high before you crash into tears for no reason. This is all normal. Have a good snotty cry, breathe and journal it out in here.

- Sex or loving on yourself! It's ok to get jiggy if you feel like it…you might even find it's the best in a while as the hormones have a surge in your body before they decide to disappear.

- ♛ Remind those around you, especially at weeks four to six, that you might look ok as time goes on, but inside you're still healing. Wounds may be small or healed but there's a lot of layers to mend underneath. I vote for four solid weeks in your PJs!

- ♛ Movement - build walking pace and distance, pelvic floor exercises when you feel ready, but follow the specific exercise routine for your type of recovery. There are some good ones online or ask a specialist.

- ♛ Keep talking. If you're thinking you might need that therapy now, it's okay, you've been through a lot.

- ♛ Book something nice for yourself to look forward to, whatever your budget. A cinema trip, some professional cleaners, whatever floats your boat.

- ♛ Comparison is not the way to healing! There will always be 'that person' that springs back, runs that marathon or breezes it back to work and that's fabulous - for them! You do your body, your mind, your feelings and your recovery. Simple!

- ♛ When you're ready to emerge back to the world of work, education or just full on play, don't underestimate having an open conversation with your boss/peers/tutor. Take full use of any phased return policies and check out Rule 11.

> I could really go on forever, but I want you to feel like you've got this right from the get go. It's up to you to find out what you need and heal in your way. You won't get it all right, no one does, but you'll learn so much.

REFLECTIONS

Reflecting on how far you've come after bidding farewell to your uterus or ovaries can be useful, so I've left some space for you to do just that when you feel the need. It might also be a good time to do the 'letter to yourself' activity in here in The Ultimate Rule section, you know, if you're bored and you've completed Netflix!

My Reflections:

Rule 5   Be Well Prepped For 'The No Ovary Club'

My Menopause, My Journal, My Rules!

Reflection Space

Hey I'm Sophie...

Choosing A Hysterectomy In Your Twenties

My story is perhaps slightly different because I chose to have a full hysterectomy due to a stage one Cancer diagnosis. They were taking my ovaries but wanted to leave my womb, thinking I'd regret my decision or might decide I'd want children later. In reality, leaving my womb and cervix to endure a third operation later down the line, or the prospect of stage two or three cancer, would have been a bigger regret for me. I feel empowered by my choice, that at twenty-three years old I managed to convince my surgeon (not that he should have needed it) that I knew my body, knew what I wanted and went on to get the outcome I needed, despite a sixty-plus year-old man spouting old fashioned crap at me about the need to have kids!

It's not easy. It's okay to feel mad, frustrated or angry that this is happening to you, it probably wasn't in your life plan and that's okay. You're not alone. It might feel like it at times but there's a whole network of us out here all wanting to help you. Talking is the best medicine and there's people willing to listen and understand.

Friendships. When you're in menopause much younger than expected your friends haven't quite caught up, so we have to share what helps us when it comes to support or even the social stuff. I think the best way friends can help is to research and become menopause aware. It would be so great if my friends understood the full list of symptoms, I just feel like they'd get it more. Surgical menopause is a long journey and if your best mates understood that sometimes you're more tired and less likely to socialise, or your mental health is taking a knock, it would be much easier to navigate.

The second best thing friends can do to support you is to just listen. Ask what your symptoms are? How are you feeling? Just listen. Be a shoulder to cry on and know that just being there for your friend is amazing. Their life has changed massively and they just need some support from those closest to them (also a box of chocolate and a bottle of wine wouldn't go amiss)! It's not over after a couple of weeks, so keep checking up and for those going through it remember friends change as you grow, so you may have to share this part of yourself multiple times.

My nugget of wisdom for the next generation: Do NOT be quiet. Do NOT pretend you're okay if you're not. You're going through a massive change to your body and personality so speak up. Make sure everyone you love knows exactly what's going on, because you need them to. Don't soldier on, there's no need. Speaking up is the only way we'll see change and get everyone more comfortable to talk about this stuff.

My top tip: find people like you who have been through similar. If you're like me and find yourself here in your twenties, it sometimes feels like the only people around feeling the same are your mum's mates and all much older, it's not much use. They're nice to chat with but they don't GET it because they aren't our age. Get on socials or join groups, connect with people in surgical menopause and find your own tribe, it'll make a world of difference.

Sophie Lauren – surgical menopause at age twenty-three Xxx

Sophie shares her experience and helps raise awareness in her workplace on:

Instragram : @surgicalmenopause23

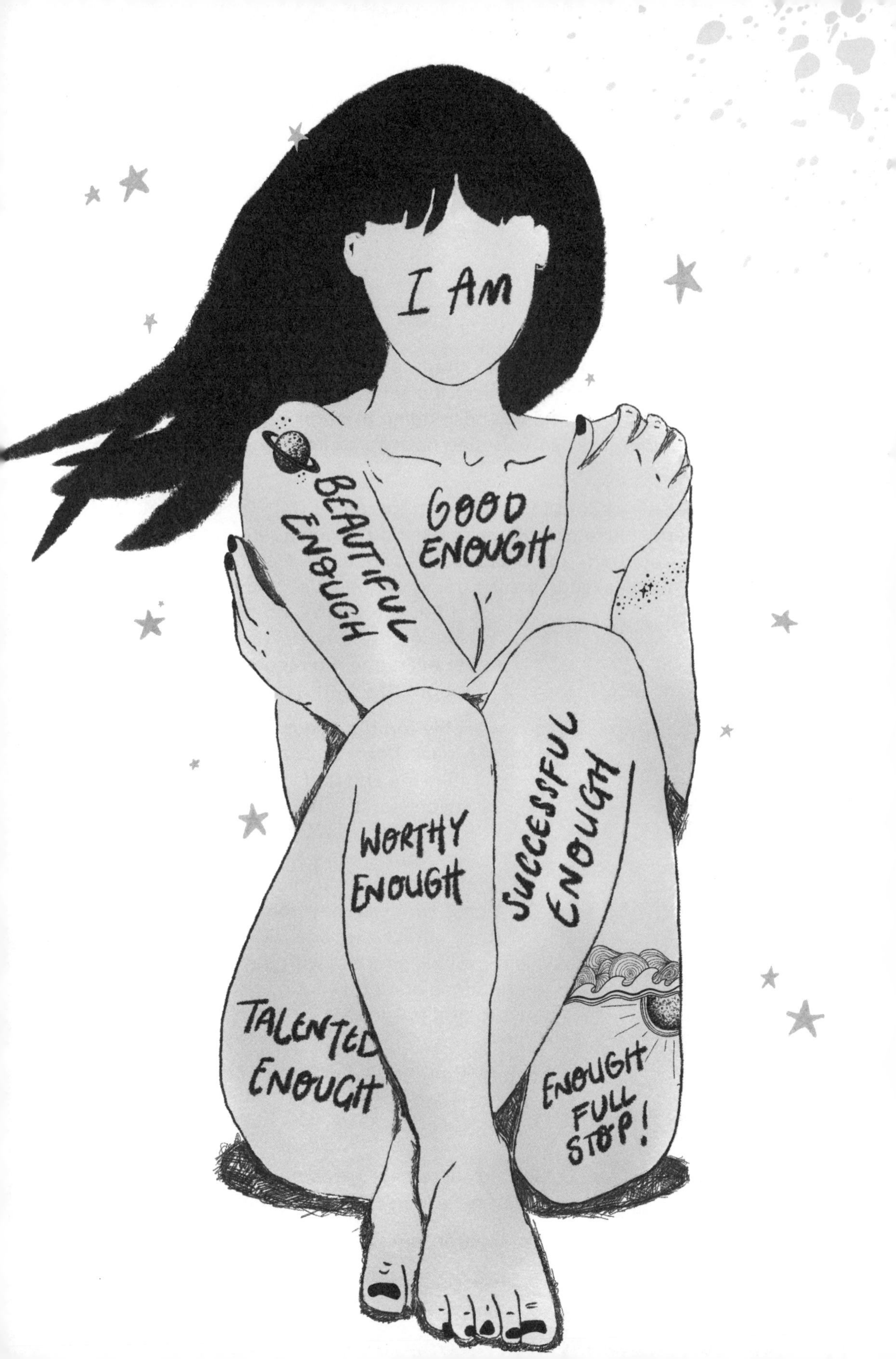
I AM
BEAUTIFUL ENOUGH
GOOD ENOUGH
WORTHY ENOUGH
SUCCESSFUL ENOUGH
TALENTED ENOUGH
ENOUGH FULL STOP!

RULE 6

love your body

If I was to include every physical symptom for this transition, we'd be here all day and you would have completed your quota of strength training just lifting this book. So, I've touched on the ones I get asked about the most and left space for you to scribble where you've swatted up on any other ailments you're feeling at the moment.

Right twiddle those chin hairs and read on...

SLEEPY HEAD

There really is nothing like a good night's sleep. It may not feel like you've had one since 2004 and everything else feels so much more difficult when we're lacking the rest. When symptoms creep in

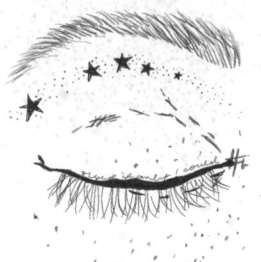

Just trying to catch some Zzzz's

our slumber is one of the first things to get disrupted. It's duvet on duvet off, leg in leg out, creating a hokey cokey ripple effect dictating how we take on the day, what we eat and how close we are to teetering on the edge of losing it. It's the vicious cycle of fatigue! I've not got the sleep thing down yet, I get the most horrendous night sweats and there's been 2 am, 3 am and 4 am overthinking raves that could create a tornado. I'm not consistent in setting myself up for a dreamy doze off...I'm just too addicted to social media. But there's no doubt when I do this stuff mentioned, I'm just that bit fresher! Along with some of the supplements I've shared, and a few things to think about around eating that you'll read in a bit, try to build these habits into your day so you can create a better way to drift off. No promises you'll stay there, but you'll be able to keep a bit saner in those times when you wake throughout the night too.

BE SLEEP READY

- Set a bedtime curfew - stick to it...mostly!
- Take a bath - not too hot or too close to bedtime will avoid the sticky heatwave aftermath.
- Switch off/do not disturb all tech an hour before bed. Screen stimulation mixed with the feelings that socials conjure is huge!
- Wear cotton, bamboo or temperature regulating nightware. Have a spare set ready to switch into if needed.
- If you're able to keep cool, a weighted blanket is amazing! Reasonably priced and cheaper than some of the whizzy gadgets that claim to aid insomnia.
- Ditch the duvet, adding thinner layers in natural fabrics.
- Journal out thoughts, lists, or ideas, so you know they're dealt with to revisit tomorrow.
- Self-Pleasure/frisky time. I know you're knackered but those feel-good hormones - such as Prolactin reducing rapid eye movement - release, giving a dreamy relaxed feeling, calm your mind and reduce anxiety whilst helping relieve physical stress. I've set myself up here when the husband reads this!
- Avoid bedroom TV - break the habit, there really is zero benefit of having one in your place of sanctuary.
- Relax your jaw - we hold tension there. Shake it out, touch your tongue to the top of your mouth hard and then slowly release.
- Learn to bedtime breathe and meditatee with guided apps, sleep playlists or white/brown noise.

Blimey, I should really take some of my own advice!

Rule 6   Love Your Body

THE 2 AM TOILET RUN!

There are some things your body does in the night that are not within your control right now. Night sweats may be preventable with tweaking the HRT or things shared already, but that wee or three you need, or if insomnia or anxiety hits, it's often how we react to these that triggers the ongoing disruption and this is something you can focus on. It's all about keeping those stress hormones in their cage by taking on the night in a calm and accepting way.

- Don't beat yourself up. If you're struggling, don't fight it.

- Avoid clock watching, it does no favours. Try to re-visit some of your pre-bedtime rituals instead.

- Avoid the screens at all costs!

- Have this book/notepad, nearby. If anxious feelings, overthinking or the impending doom lurks, write it out.

- Anxiety - focus on your breathing, check out some techniques in Rule 8.

- Have a sleep meditation ready - no clearing your mind needed, it's ok to think, hear the clock or want to smother your snoring partner with a pillow! Acknowledge it all.

- Toilet runs - it is what it is. A hallway plug light keeps you semi sleepy. As you wee, close your eyes...relax, breathe. Sounds weird but distracts from the 'FFS frustration' that your body is doing this to you.

- Panic - if you've tried preventive practises and your HRT is on point, do you have allergies? This could be histamine playing havoc with your Estrogen. Try an anti-histamine an hour before bed.

Rule 6   Love Your Body

Note down anything you've tried that was helpful to remind yourself of is you need:

Rule 6 Love Your Body

My Menopause, My Journal, My Rules!

MIDNIGHT THOUGHTS:

Rule 6　Love Your Body

FOOD... NOM NOM NOM

Fact: I'm probably closer to touring with Beyonce than I am to being a nutritionist. I have a severe biscuit addiction, with the ability to scoff a whole packet of chocolate digestives in one sitting! Now, everyone will have a take on their relationship between food and hormones depending on dietary needs, culture or budget. If someone was cooking me fully balanced meals daily, could I be sugar-free, macro-aware and perfectly portioned, even in those times when I want to dive into the chocolate like Augustus Gloop? Maybe. But instead I'm cooking for four, three different dinners, in times where I'm so exhausted I can't remember where an egg comes from, with the budget for baked beans on toast. So, forgive me if the grocery shop, along with the concept of what food to inhale, tips me over the edge.

Mix diet cultures with hormone balancing concepts, varying opinions and how palatable your needs are for a smoothie lightly dusted with the rare sperm of the Amazon tree frog and my mind is blown. Let's be honest, all I want to do is eat the cake when the chips are down! I have, however, learnt that consuming twenty creme eggs in five days and living purely on sour dough, butter and jam is not the way forward in terms of keeping my gut in top condition to have a fighting chance against this hormone battle. It's a no brainer that whatever gender we are, in any stage of life, fuelling our bodies cleanly will have a positive impact.

With that in mind, I'm keeping this short with what has worked for me at this particular stage of my life. No hard and fast diet plans included... there is no quick fix peeps, there just isn't. You've got to start listening to your own body.

It took me a long time to work out I need to let go of the diet thing, brought up when 'heroin chic' was what my teenage self was aspiring too, says it all. However, what has come more recently with my ever-changing chubby bits is a wisdom, that my body in itself has been through so much. So, before the food got a look in, I had to do some work on wanting to nourish it because of love. Not because I was trying to squeeze into a pair of denims that I'd held on to from my pre-op days!

Buying the bigger jeans is ok...believe me, you'll look and feel so much better. Wear the clothes that make you feel a thousand smiles, the ones you can eat a proper lunch in and still feel fab. Do this before you even think about the food stuff!

When I can be bothered, meal prepping helps me budget and plan (so overthinking doesn't holler) and keeps me on track to feel great, however, 1) there's so many plans available for so many differing needs, 2) some carry the guilt of that weekend chocolate, wine or full on buffet...so again it's time to look at this as the rest of your life. If like me, you're planning on staying around for while – blimey you may have diced with death before – why the hell are we reprimanding ourselves over a piece of Victoria sponge? Delve into the food business if you wish, find a trusted nutritionist, allergy consultant, sugar coach, whatever floats your biscuit if you feel the need.

What you need to put in your stomach depends on your food preferences, medical needs such as diabetes, or allergies or culture. I find simplicity helps, so here's some things to remember day to day that will help your overall feeling of being a little more in harmony with your hormones in terms of food.

Every meal should have:

Protein – Helps muscles stay strong, gives sustained energy, keeps us full and helps those sugar cravings.

Good fats (not saturated) – Good heart health and glowing skin. Think olive/coconut oil, Avocado, Flax/Chia seeds in a smoothie or salad or coconut milk in those fresh curries.

Carbs – Yes, eat the sweet potato, that jacket potato with tuna mayo or basmati rice, just don't eat a pile bigger than your palm and keep it clean. If the bread brings you joy, without discomfort, enjoy!

Rule 6   Love Your Body

As a child of the 80s, cereal and toast was the breakfast staple. A total morning sugar spike from the get-go. Think more eggs on toast with avocado or oats with some protein powder and a bit of nut butter. That type of shizzle will start your day a little more balanced.

Eating clean, means trying to remove anything additional that is added for our convenience! Eating clean does not mean 100 per cent of the time. It means doing what you can when you can. If you're on a focused plan for a while, take each day at a time. When you start to re-introduce things, watch for changes…what do you notice? For example, when my energy was so low I struggled to function, I did a thirty day gut reset, removing gluten, alcohol and dairy. I ate lean protein, took supplements with added pea protein powders, loads of fresh colourful foods, with tons of greens. I also ate eighty-five per cent chocolate every day.

I felt amazing, it controlled my sugar cravings and I started to see my vulva again. Once I finished I introduced gluten back in and immediately saw changes in my skin as small red spots appeared! Dairy flipped my stomach out and I'd feel lethargic. Since then, if it's easy to make a kinder choice I'll go there. If the lemon meringue pie is calling, I'll still go there, but I'm in tune enough to not dive all in for days on end. I'm learning to respect that my body deserves more than that.

Here's some other pointers:

- ✓ Avoid added sugar before twelve noon
- ✓ Look for good quality pea protein with added vitamins to add to smoothies or oats
- ✓ Soya has Estrogen in it!
- ✓ Fresh vegan snacks are a good go to in coffee shops, even if you're not vegan
- ✓ Switch to gluten free pasta or pizza bases
- ✓ A banana before bed if you must snack, it helps with sleep
- ✓ Add greens to everything

NOTE

I learnt from menopause coach Amantha King that we have receptors for Estrogen in our bodies and those receptors happen to be the same place that Histamine lives too. These two things work like twins within us. So, when the Estrogen levels drop our Histamine is like 'oh come on' going into overdrive trying to increase our Estrogen levels. This is why allergies can start or become worse in menopause! This was a mic drop moment. Histamine is not just in pollen, it's found in food too like strawberries, chocolate and coffee (is there no joy?). It's particularly high in anything that grows above the ground but below our knees. Hard when you're filling the bowl with nutritional salads leaves and peppers. We need this colourful food stuff, so if you're noticing you're reacting take an anti-histamine on waking. I couldn't get over what a difference it made when I ditched eating so many strawberries first thing in the morning. If you're an allergy sufferer, I highly recommend researching the effects of Histamine and what other foods it's in - the list is ridiculous! You might need to change up medication if you're flaring or breaking out in allergic reactions that you didn't have before.

RUNNING ON CAFFEINE

Some experts say that caffeine can worsen symptoms such as hot flushes and night sweats. This is because our blood vessels react, and our bodies try to regulate. However, caffeine does have some positive effects too: increasing concentration, helping over-all wellbeing and lifting your mood. I used to run on sugared coffee with a biscuit dunked in, but now have one caffeinated coffee a day and make sure it's before twelve noon so it's out of my system by bedtime, however I've substituted it first thing with a natural Ginko booster to avoid the 7 am fake surge. My tummy prefers oat or almond milk and I like a fresh good quality one over instant. It's a mindful moment of my day as I enjoy the ritual of making it, taking time to de-stress while drinking – outside if I can or in my favourite chair. It also gets things moving in the poo department! I drink water, decaf or peppermint tea for the rest of the day. It's all in the small changes, so remember...

- ✓ Caffeine before twelve noon but not on waking
- ✓ Switch to decaf coffee/tea
- ✓ Try fresh sage tea - tastes like shit, but may help hot flushes

LET'S TALK ABOUT H2O -

You're not drinking enough, so drink more...simple!

Learn to love the weight your body has carried...not the weight it holds on its bones. The weight you have carried is far more significant than the weight around your waist.

Rule 6   Love Your Body

LAST ORDERS! - ALCOHOL

I'm not even going to tell you to stop the alcohol...there I've said it! I love a tequila or espresso martini when the dance floor is calling and there's been times when a bottle of vino has literally saved a few people from being murdered! You're an adult, you know the deal, so maybe just make a note of how your differing tipples affect your symptoms. If you can find one that leaves you less sweaty than a rugby player, hurrah! For example, red wine brings me night sweats from hell and because of its high Histamine level I'm bunged up to the eyeballs and look like Rudolph. As a rule, wine is probably the worst and spirits like gin are less chaotic in terms of Histamine or symptom starters.

Try a few non-alcoholic alternatives, there are so many now. Some are grim and overpriced so weigh it up, but what's the harm in drinking a few mocktails in between the real deal? Often it's about the atmosphere and even the glass that creates that feeling we crave, so play about with that.

Reducing alcohol tips:

- ✓ Drink water in between rounds
- ✓ Get the pretty glasses out. How we dress up the drink is just as important as what's in it! Make it fancy; ice, garnish and a rocking glass makes a huge difference to feeling included when everyone else is getting shit-faced
- ✓ Try Kombucha - it's a little bitter, but there's various flavours such as ginger, rhubarb and even mojito. It's really good for your gut!
- ✓ Stand your ground - often others have more of a problem with us not drinking than us ourselves. Put yourself first and remember why you don't want to feel a hormonal mess for days

If you do feel that your relationship with this stuff is not as healthy as you'd like, and you're thinking maybe you'd like to try the sober life, that's awesome. Invest some time to chat to someone; GP, charities, or a sober coach, there are people out there to help you make the first positive steps.

KITCHEN DANCER, DOG-WALKER – MOVE THAT BODY

For some of you, active wear will be a staple of your style, banging out the burpees and lifting the kg's, or navigating a downward dog yoga pose on a paddle board. For some, 1,500 might be your average step count and the only crunch you're doing is to pick up all the washing around the house, or you may be (like me) somewhere in between. You are where you are, for whatever reason, but whether you love or loathe exercise, let's agree with what's on the post-it!

I'm a mixed bag. When my anxiety buggers off and I can enter a gym, I'm all over lifting a few weights or doing a class where I can punch like I'm smacking the goollies out of my rage. I quite like to jog (not really with people, they're annoying), with a good podcast or playlist and I do walk the dog a lot. There have been times when I've been all in at 5 am and times when my depression moved me no further than my front door, it ebbs and flows and that's ok. Remember that one per cent? That's all you need in helping to keep this vessel of yours carrying you stronger and sassier and, quite frankly, going 100 per cent is rather dangerous, as I learned that time I entered a spin studio!

Movement is good... any movement is in fact great for you in menopause!

From the minute I sat on the saddle (clearly made for someone with no arse), I realised I'd made a school girl error! It was a beginner's class so I persisted, questioning **what's the worst that can happen?** Which is kind of ironic, as our family mantra to this question is...'you could die!'

Let me paint you a picture. I thrashed my legs as my new sizeable boobs (thanks Progesterone) whacked my three chins only to rebound downwards onto my mid-section, where my menopausal 'gunt' (that merge of gut and paunchy nether bits) ricocheted against my thighs. As if this wasn't enough, the skinny saddle was too high, and my vulva pounded it like a clapping sea-lion in distress.

Spinning - motivational my arse, in fact I didn't feel my arse for three weeks!

I didn't go back.

I guess what I'm saying is I'm more of a kitchen dancer. Stick on the tunes, get on the table and twerk enough to embarrass the kids. Keep cardio healthy and tone your booty all at once kind of girl. Kitchen dancing is my kind of movement and it's fun! So find something that lights you up and move a little more than you usually do.

However, there is some stuff around movement we really should think about incorporating into the funky club of menopause: 1) weight training and 2) flexibility. Get creative at home or go and seek the experts exploring how you can mix these two things into your week on top of cardio. Here's why:

Weight training – Creates strong lean muscle which protects and keeps bones healthy. Something we all need especially as decreased Estrogen means decreased muscle mass and an added risk of osteoporosis. Small weights or body weight is fine. Unless you're lifting heavy with low reps, you're not going to bulk up – fact!

Getting Supple – Simple stretches, Yoga or Pilates, help balance the body, mind and soul. It's stress reducing and makes getting out of bed a whole lot easier with those aching joints.

Cardio – Walking at pace, skipping, getting the roller skates on or kicking a football round the garden, whatever makes you smile, raising your heart rate a smidge more than usual is like investing in Apple in the 90s!

Love the skin you're in

okay, but what if it's attached to my left boob touching the floor?

CONSCIOUS CONNECTED BREATHWORK

Everything comes from our breath, it's running the show of our bodies, it's life and yet we pay so little attention to it. So, I wanted to dabble with breathwork and understand its power. Not to be mistaken for meditation, this practise can be intense, emotional and can take you out of your comfort zone. It's great that this ancient craft is finding its way into modern lives and lingo. You might be thinking that I've made a booboo putting breathwork in this section and not in the one all about our minds. I've touched on the lighter breathwork practises there in more detail, but there is a reason that the deep stuff is here, this is conscious connected breathing.

The power of breath has the ability to relax or energise and has been linked to help things like brain fog, anxiety, fatigue and hot flushes but also aching joints and inflammation, and if done consistently has the ability to tap into a deeper intuition! It's far more than cold showers and ice baths (which can set you up for the day). The deeper work has a longer lasting affect – sometimes for weeks. It's controlling the air travelling through, yet it may also feel like you're fighting your brain, because it's much more intense than the surface level breathwork you may be familiar with. This is because you're really tapping into the route of your nervous system to release much deeper stuff within you. It's physical to do and its benefits run throughout the body as a whole.

If you're looking for this full on experience, look out for a qualified breath coach that should be asking for waivers to be signed beforehand and explaining any risks to you personally, for example this can be risky for those with heart issues or if you've recently had surgery, so it's important to do your research beforehand. This makes it all sound very scary, it isn't I promise, but our bodies can do strange things when we go deep into our breath, so it's good to be aware.

So, my verdict on the full on session? Wow, it's hard work and I'm not going to pretend I loved the experience. I struggled to allow my body to settle in and release, it was like my head got in the way, saying this is just not normal, despite that being kind of the point! The after glow I got after just one session however was lovely, I was extremely relaxed. I'm just not that great yet at trusting myself and my body fully to give in... I'm not one to give up, so I'll be giving it another go, because the benefits of this in menopause far outweigh my fear of not being in control.

FIND THE FLOW

Rule 6   Love Your Body

Hey I'm Amy...

'You Don't Look Old Enough to be in Menopause,'

At 27 I was diagnosed with premature ovarian insufficiency (POI), after an emergency operation to remove two large ovarian cysts and one ovary. My remaining ovary didn't recover from the trauma of surgery and my periods never came back. Instead, crippling menopause symptoms appeared and I went from feeling like a vibrant, young, bubbly woman to frumpy, achy, tearful and broken. A diagnosis came nine months after surgery, along with my first dose of hormones, it was such a relief to receive both. I felt like I had an answer, validation and relief washing over me when the HRT kicked in.

Before my diagnosis I never really heard about, or understood, the fullness of menopause, believing it was just the end of a woman's periods. I was never aware of how it was essentially a long-term hormone deficiency. Only after my own research and education did I understand the long-term benefits of me, a young woman, being on HRT. I learnt the undeniable fact that Estrogen fuels a woman's body and without the sufficient levels for our age we are hot messes – literally!

Menopause should matter we need to change the face of it. It's not just older grey haired women, it's bright, ambitious and determined young women too!

What if I'd been more educated in this stuff? I do look back a lot about how life could have been different. How I might still have my fertility if women's health was a key part of education. How I might not have ingrained thoughts about my body failing me, if I was taught about fertility issues and menopause at school...what if? I wish gynae issues including POI and menopause weren't so taboo, with more education and awareness so women can identify symptoms and not suffer in silence before it's potentially too late.

My nuggets of wisdom – to anyone, but particularly my generation and the next – are to know your family's gynaecological history issues and to those of you being asked, please be honest and open. It might sound intense and may be awkward, but I wish I'd known that my grandmother and mum had similar monster-sized cysts, that caused havoc for them under the age of thirty.

Three women, same family, all who have experienced ovary removal or even a full hysterectomy.

So, is it genetic? Maybe, the only proof is the patterns we can see. Who knows if my surgery could have been avoided, if doctors observed that pattern and included questions about family history alongside ones like, 'what contraception are you on?' or 'is there a possibility you're pregnant?' which are asked so easily and, even for me now, can be heartbreaking.

Find your community. For me I went to the Daisy Network, a charity dedicated to helping women with the diagnosis of POI. Finding a community on social media of people just like me has been awesome. I then found purpose in the pain by sharing my story, creating menopause memes in the hope to empower, empathise and hopefully entertain those experiencing or learning.

Amy Fleming POI at twenty-seven years old XXX

Amy shares her POI journey with such humour and fun, I love her! Find her on:

Instagram: @girl_poiwer

TikTok: @Girl_POIwer

BREAST TO IMPRESS

Breasts, boobs, tits, puppies, jugs, tatties, golf balls in socks, gnat bites, bee stings or mammaries. Swinging low or standing firm, whatever you call them, however and in whichever direction they may appear to be protruding from your chest, if you have them, then any hormonal changes mean these beauties are going to feel it and sometimes react. Mine have felt like they've doubled in size at times, been tender and sore as I've played about with different medications, and I've had the old 'chub rub' happen as they've bouldered about in an ill-fitting sports bra! They ballooned quite rapidly just recently whilst I adjusted to Progesterone tablets. My back was suddenly thinking 'what the...?', as it now tried to master this added weight on top of the middle mass I also seem to have grown.

I actually weighed my left boob once... I kid you not. Leaning down tactically placing my left melon upon the scales. 'ERROR' it shouted. 'FFS' I thought, that means I really am carrying that three stone of excess weight somewhere else!

CHECK THOSE BOOBS

The thing is this part of our body does change as the hormones manoeuvre and it's important to take note of anything different. If you feel something unusual it can feel extremely scary. I was quickly referred to my first visit to a breast cancer clinic after finding a lump, and waiting to go in I had a thousand catastrophising thoughts, before finally having a word with my rationale self and realising I'm probably not alone in thinking all this. Thankfully the lump was a fatty cyst and they explained hormonal changes could do this from time to time.

Being in menopause so much younger meant they liked to take precautions. I would be welcome at the clinic any time to get checked over, which felt a relief. I made a promise to check more regularly.

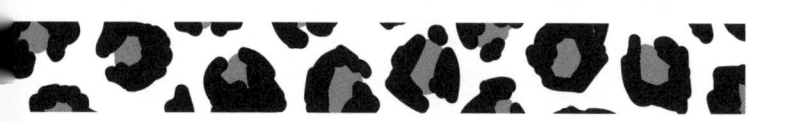

WHEN TO CHECK:

Monthly – and it's good to check around the same time, this takes into account menstrual cycles, hormone changes etc. which can make things tender, a bit harder or lumpy. It's also good to make a mental note if you've started any different medication or supplements.

Brain fog reminder! It's good to set yourself a nudge, time flies and it's easier to forget with everything else on your plate. Use your phone, fridge note, stick it on your calendar or mark a 'B' for Boobs on your HRT packet/the last patch of the month or pump pack, crossing out when you've had a prod and poke.

Go on... go and do it, set your reminder somewhere.

☐ Tick the box once done!

HOW DO I CHECK THEM?

Any checking is better than none, there's no wrong way to do it as they're your breasts. The more you do it the more you're able to know what's normal for you. Feel, press and roll your hand over and around. Go right from underneath the breast, over and around, up to your collar bone and under your armpit (don't forget to lift your arm up) – this is all classed as breast tissue.

You're looking for soreness that is particularly painful, inverted nipples, lumps, swelling or any predominant changes in size. If you notice anything, monitor it for a week and if no change, visit your GP.

Rule 6   Love Your Body

HRT AND BREAST CANCER RISKS

There is a lot of gumph (formal word for out-of-date research and scare-mongering) written around links to HRT and breast cancer. It can all feel very confusing and of course we should always remember that how it is for one person could be very different to another. I've shared how I feel about stats, so I won't add any here, but if you are teetering on the edge of not taking HRT because you're worried, I urge you to go and check out the most recent professional views on what the actual numbers are (they may not be as scary as you think). Get the facts that are right for your specific situation. Research your specific breast cancer links, you may find a low dosage Estrogen might be a choice you didn't realise you had! However we should always check our baps!

HOT MESSES

It's not all about flushes, but goodness they are like the heat that comes from lava and I might get backlash if I don't give them a little section. As they wash over suddenly it can feel like your skin is hot enough to fry an egg on. They're often the first sign that something hormonal is changing and can totally ruin your look and mood as one fires up just as you're about to walk out the door looking glamorous. As mentioned, HRT and the alternatives can help, along with choosing natural clothing or something a bit looser. There might be times when you want to frolic in the snow in a bikini or stand naked in front of your open fridge, do it! The embarrassment of hot flushes can strike anywhere; as you swipe your customer's shopping through, the kid in your class questions why you're sweating, or you're at that very important event in that outfit you've longed to wear for so long.

Don't be afraid to explain what is happening and remember sweat patches are normal, it's just society that has told us otherwise. Wear layers rather than chunky clothing and carry a handy fan. I love the roller ball I keep in the freezer, run my wrists under cold water and have a funky little bamboo cloth to blot that face. Hair up if you suffer around your neck and politely ask whoever is in the vicinity to just give you a minute as it passes.

SKIN DEEP

Acne, red blotches, rosacea, hives, itching and dryness, oh, and that wonderful thing that is dull and ageing wrinkles. No matter what we may tell ourselves, society's view of what we **should** look like is literally smacking us in the face on the daily. As someone who suffered horrendously with hormonal acne, to the point where my face was covered in purple boils and was so painful to touch, I tried everything before investing in a dermatologist who put me on Roaccutane. This isn't for sissies and was a last resort for me, but it changed my life after just six months. I now use mainly natural products on my face, spending only what I can afford.

- Hydrate with water from within
- Organic coconut oil for dry itching bodies
- Try copying face yoga videos
- Think about your gut, is research linked to your particular issue?
- Slap on SPF always!
- Remember filters are fuckwits! Whether you're into an oats and coconut oil mask or Botox, your face is your face so do whatever makes you feel good. There are creams and potions that are aimed at menopause and we've heard about peptides and collagen on all the adverts. However, these are only surface level and often any skin issues come from a direct internal root cause, so keep exploring.

HAIR TODAY, GONE TOMORROW

I come from a good line of beard growers. My Dad literally is Santa and I'm coming fast up the ranks in terms of growing my own forest from my chin. Where the hell does that bad boy come from, popping up an inch long? Whether side of face, straight out the areola or off the shoulder, they often leaving me thinking *how did I not notice this before* and wondering why hasn't anyone bothered to mention my new best mate? Plucking these little friends has become part of my make-up routine in a well-lit space!

- Avoid dermaplaning. I know we want rid of the peach fuzz, but it could worsen things when your hormones fluctuate or you are on HRT

- Thread, wax, pluck, even laser, but even hair removal creams can irritate menopausal sensitive skin

- Or say fuck it, add some glitter and rock that beard!

JUST WHEN YOU THINK YOU'VE GOT IT ALL FIGURED OUT...

that single, black, pube like hair appears out of no-where on your face and makes you realise that you **DON'T HAVE ALL THE ANSWERS.**

Our locks on our head however are not about vanity. They are our expression of who we are, so when things start to thin or fall it can feel really distressing. Supplements may help a little, diet too but essentially when Estrogen drops and hereditary factors come to play, it's more tricky. There is research being done all the time for treatments like PRP (platelet-rich-plasma), where your own blood/plasma is injected back in the scalp, and micro-pigmentation, becoming more mainstream. These can be expensive though and you need to seek out the right professionals, acting fairly quickly before hair follicles become too weak.

- Not overheating your hair with irons/curlers

- Avoiding sulphates in all hair products

- Tying hair up loosely can avoid additional strain.

- Vitamin D and special topical treatments could also help

- Scalp brushing

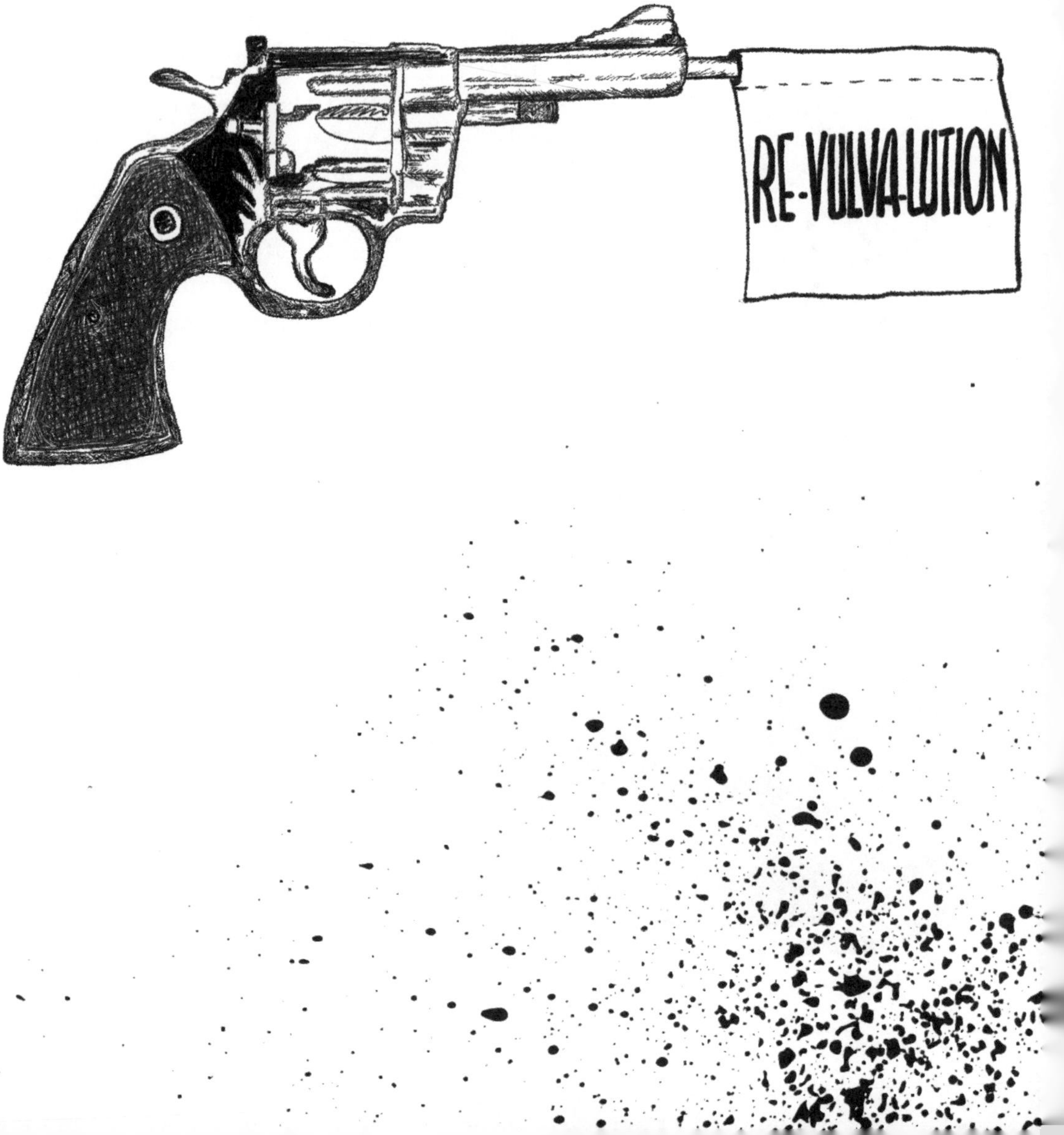
RE-VULVA-LUTION

RULE 7

START A Re-Vulva-lution

GIVE YOUR PUSSY POWER – ARE YOU CRINGING?

Are you ready for it? We're going there. Time to focus on the power of the pussy...yours to be exact. Here's the crux, we're really good at hiding things especially when it comes to what's happening 'down there'. Blimey, we often struggle to even say the words VAGINA and VULVA out loud, let alone chat to our mates about, how ours is feeling as a dry as a box of Wetabix from 1985! And if you're wondering why I've mentioned vagina and vulva, aren't they the same thing? It's because nope, they aren't the same thing

The vagina is your love tunnel dear, and the vulva incorporates the rest. The outside, the bits we see. It's quite incredible that along with the menopause, this also seems to have bypassed us as something we should *actually* be aware of! What's even **more** incredible is that there isn't a definitive word that encapsulates the whole thing. It's no wonder we're left somewhere in-between: quietly mouthing 'down there,' telling our kids to cover their flower, minnies or foofs, and then trying to reclaim the word pussy or cunt. We hear so much about loss of libido in menopause and I get asked a lot, 'will I ever orgasm the same after my hysterectomy?' I feel it's time to really address some of the things testosterone just won't fix! I really believe that understanding more about this powerful part of us is a huge rite of passage towards something fiercely liberating – in whatever way we're taking on menopause and the years beyond.

Also be under no illusion how this connection will cast a web backwards to the generations to come who are already far more in tune with their own pussy power than I have ever been. So, get ready for this section it's a big one and it requires an open mind. But there's a reason it's included which will all become clear...be brave!

I'm far from a guru in this area. Believe me, thirty-three smear tests from the age of fifteen to thirty-three, two decades of Endometriosis, extremely painful sex, one highly traumatic premature birth, PTS, and a tear that was stitched up wrong (so we had to go again for a designer vagina), has left my sacred yoni somewhat traumatised! I'm not kidding when I say, there must have been over 150 pairs of 'medical eyes' that have looked between my legs. So, forgive me for wanting to close my knees, squint my eyes, hold tight and hang on, as surgical menopause hit and I wondered what the hell it was going to serve my lady garden! There are, of course (as we've established earlier), symptoms associated with how this part of our body might react to the changes that menopause brings, which are really important to be aware of, but can we really be comfortable tackling symptoms properly, or preventing them, if we can't even say what we call it proudly?

In my own quest to learning about myself what became hugely apparent was that our sacred pelvic area holds so much more in terms of its energy. This is an important factor and our beautiful selves are worthy of not only talking biological symptoms, but leaning into that energy and re-connecting!

IT'S NOT ALL SCREAMING ORGASMS...

As I sat with my friend Tania Nishi (who happens to be known as 'The Naked Coach') I was hoping she would download her expertise through a few pointers to help pass on to you. What I wasn't expecting was to uncover and truly immerse into my own thoughts and an inner dialogue, that hasn't ever surfaced before – and it was powerful. So be prepared to not only get under the skin, but around all its juicy (or not so) parts. Because before we try to soothe the symptoms or lift libido, we need to get a little deep with that energy, open our heart and mind honestly and even face some past trauma. We need to do the work!

> LOVE NOTE: if you're not quite ready for this bit, or it's bringing stuff up, you have full permission to skip ahead to the more practical side of pelvic health. You do you and you're welcome back to this place when, or if the time feels right. It goes without saying that whilst giving you a flavour of myself and Tania's conversation, if anything we uncover takes you to a place beyond where these pages help, remember there are professionals out there, coaches and therapists that can help you specifically.

If we're good to go, let's get fruity...

WHY IS SELF-PLEASURE AT THE BOTTOM OF THE LIST?

Write down what you do for self care? Remember 'showering' does not count!

When asked this, I spilled out the usual walking, dancing, socialising, maybe a massage if I'm lucky!

Yoni -
A source of energy,
An origin, a spring fountain.
A place of rest, a home,
A receptacle thrown.
It is the womb, vagina
And all that surrounds,
The form of our existence,
A devine procreative energy,
Encapsulating wisdom,
Expanding power from within,
She is sacred.

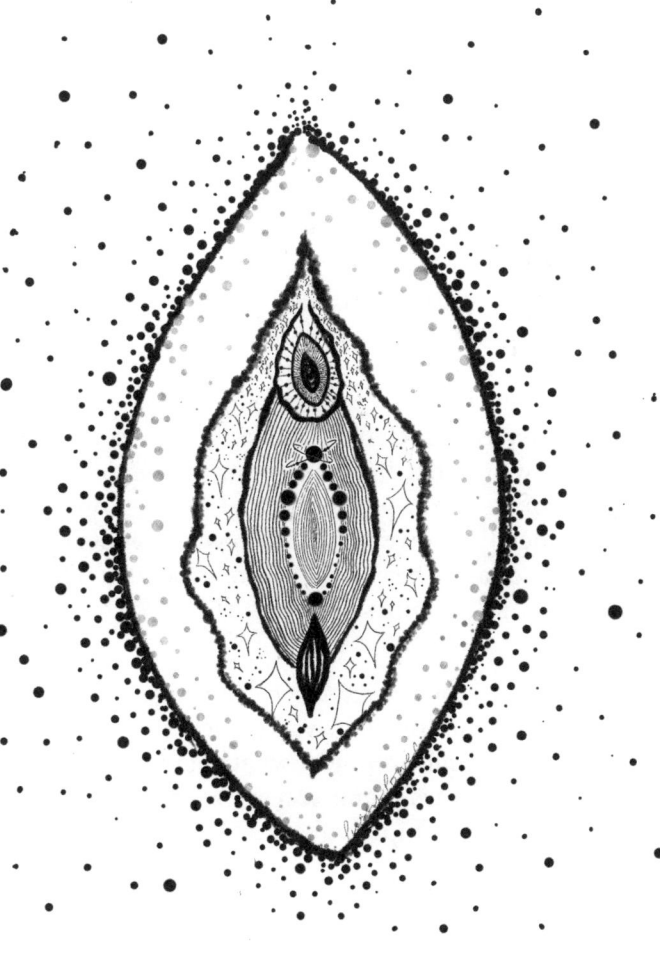

'Now, tell me what's made you associate these things with self care,' Tania asked. Hmmm... my mind started to find the answers.

What's your answer to this question?

In the conversation of life, we've learned to do what's associated with the least amount of shame. So, it's understandable why the 'go to' for self replenishment are things like the gym, binging TV shows, or buying that thing, you know 'because we're worth it!'. These all release a certain amount of endorphins, often have almost zero shame attached to them and, in fact, are usually encouraged. For most of us, pleasure from that sacred place of ours has never been part of that conversation. From the oppression of women to lack of knowledge, this abashment worked its way through mainstream society so much so, we even struggle to say the words associated with what lies within our pelvis out loud; let alone it bringing us one of its main purposes...joy! We're slowly heading in the right direction socially, however we do have a tendency as humans to jump from 'A' to 'Z' and then fumble back-tracking. This is our chance to plug in to some self compassion with this area before we plug in to anything else!

Shaving your legs in the shower is probably part of your routine, but it was really only a hundred odd years back that this was starting to become 'normal'. The conditioning of what society thought about shaving changed over a few decades from: seen as weird if you removed hair, to now paying someone to whip it all off being totally accepted and even required!

We need to understand that what lies within our pelvis isn't just biology, it's magic, requiring a lot of energy and love. We have the ability to change the outlook to more acceptance, just like it did for our silky smooth pins.

CHANGING THE CONDITIONING

Like we need good food and movement, connection to this part of us is just as crucial to our health and wellbeing. Wait what? I know right, drop the vibrator moment! Trouble is the stigma has stifled our relationship with it. We don't know what it looks like, what it feels like, we don't show it love.

Whilst drafting out this chapter, I shared it with friends to catch a vibe on the embarrassment levels. All wanting to remain on the Christmas card list, they were fully supportive, but I noticed a common theme. One of my closest friends hit the nail on the head saying, 'I love everything you've written, but I just can't say that word Pussy!' It seems the 'ick' factor of certain words is still there, why is that?

BEFORE we think about RE-CONNECTING, we need to UNDERSTAND the DISCONNECT.

Tania Nishi

WHAT DO YOU CALL YOURS?

There's no wrong or right here. I'll go first, some of mine have been: lady garden, pussy, down there, pain station, shit show and good old vajayjay and yoni, depending on who I'm talking to. Think about or list all the names you use to describe your bits and pieces or names as a whole. Now think about the words you use and start to see which one's fill the gaps as you work through the next questions.

My...

Tania went on, asking me to think about any times I felt shameful about this part of my body? I immediately tensed as instinctively I felt, 'oh there are so many'. I looked at Tania's comforting face as I realised just how unhealthy my relationship still was. How much negative emotions swirled around: feeling like a long-term medical experiment, the lack of respect I'd shown myself at times, an ill equipped baby carrier from miscarriages and not being able to hold my children full term.

It was also a place of doom and a source of such physical pain. My feelings softened as she went on to ask, 'When have you felt the opposite, connected or even powerful?' For the first time, I allowed myself to remember when I **was** aligned. How animalistic yet empowered I felt during my second childbirth, a million miles away from the trauma of the first. How in tune I was with my sexuality during a rare time of no physical pain, yet this immediately retracted back into the former disconnect of feeling dangerous and uncontrollable! I was barely scratching the surface and later revisited these questions...I still do today. But in that moment, I could see that building a new relationship to my yoni was not going to be easy.

As you answer these questions, let it all out as it comes, if you can. You may want to re-visit later too, like me. This is deep and may trigger some past experiences, so go at your own pace.

*If this raises thoughts that may feel difficult or you need support, it's okay. Take a moment to breathe, doing what feels right. Whether that's stop and make a cuppa or seek some professional help.

What has your relationship been with your [...] up to now?*

Jot down anything you can remember that felt shameful when thinking about that part of you* — education/biological/experiences:

Was there ever a time that you did feel connected? That you felt you had a good relationship?*

. . . .

. . . .

. . . .

. . . .

. . . .

. . . .

. . . .

. . . .

. . . .

. . . .

. . . .

. . . .

. . . .

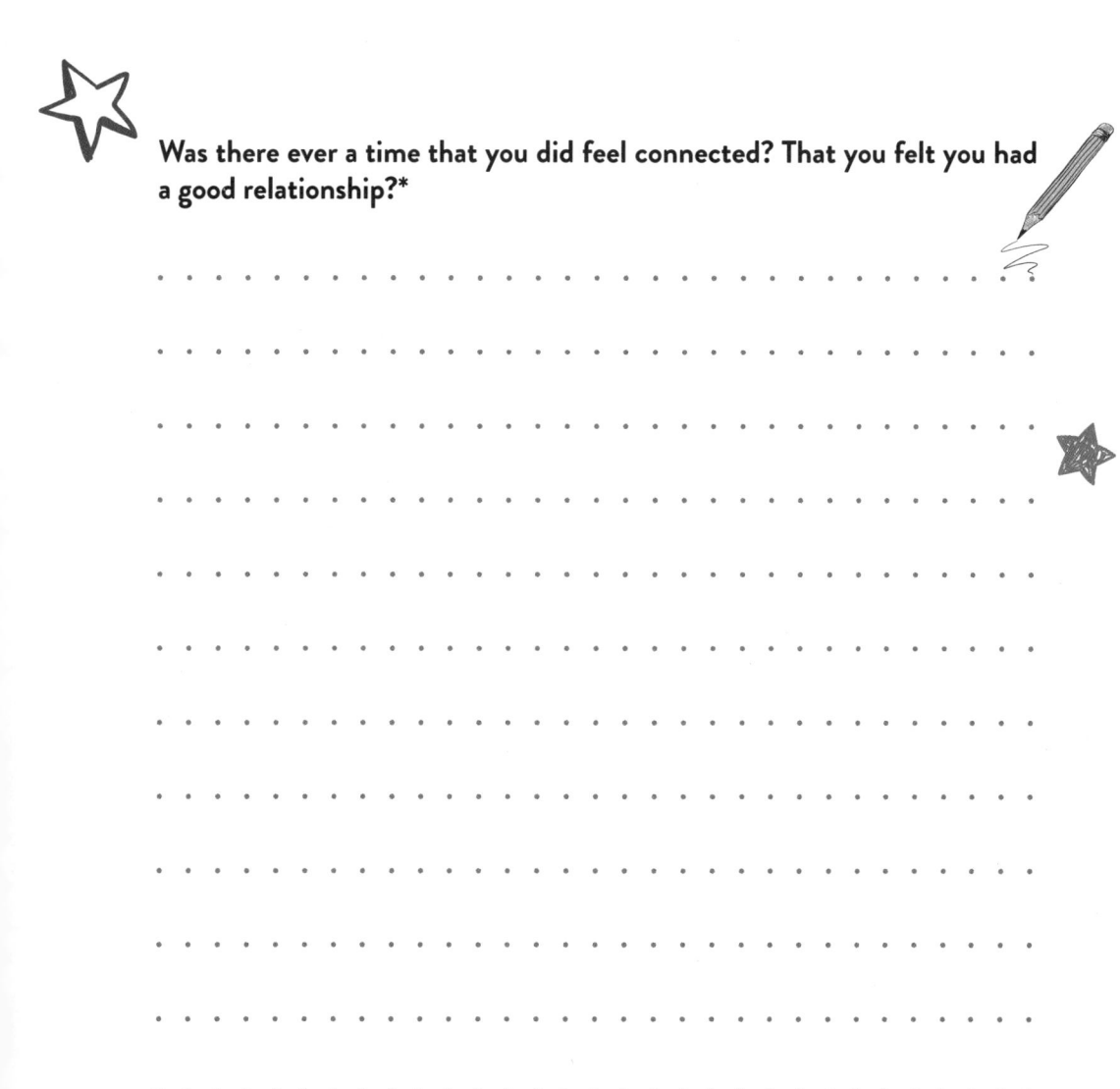

TIME TO RE-WIRE

Our relationship with our pussy, translates to our whole body. What we say about it, or to it (outwardly or internally), what we feel about how it looks or feels, literally sends messages through our wiring within. Similar to how we're programmed to think we should dress or have our hair a certain way, we've often got idealisms as to what our vulva should look like too.

What do you think re-connecting with your [...] means for you? This could be anything from simply looking in the mirror at yourself to passionate pleasure.

Does my vulva offend you?

For years we've been sent off down a path of thinking that the vulva is the vagina, the labia fitted in somewhere and the clitoris...well! Not until the early 2000s when medical journals were finally updated did the slow correction start which has gained traction more recently in things actually being called out for what they are to crush the shame. This historic backlog of terrible sex education, from rhino's shagging to a naked family from the 70s playing volleyball, to full blown childbirth, never really showed the vulva at it best nor did it allow us to have a useful opinion about them.

What do you think about vulvas?
Write or doodle what you perceive as a 'normal' vulva too look like. Think about what your reference points are, such as biological diagrams or porn. I know I'm asking a lot here, but go for it!

Now think about your entire body, what is your relationship like with that? Purge your thoughts here, however they come.

Did you write anything negative? You did?

NOW TAKE ALL THAT NEGATIVITY AND FUCK IT ALL OFF!

At this point Tania and I were laughing, waving our hands all bouchée like, 'Fuck that fucking shit right off!' She then shared just how important it is to start the cycle of letting this stuff go, before we can truly move onto her slow and steady steps to realignment.

Any negative opinions you've written above are just not serving you or your pussy!

Later in Rule 9, you'll be introduced to the 'Fuck it bucket ritual' where you get to let go of some stuff with fire! You may want to come back here and add these feelings to that activity if it helps. I'm completely aware though that years of body issues aren't going to just disappear with a burnt piece of paper and a couple of mantras, as we said at the top, this is work, it's ongoing. However, there is something beautifully liberating in making a mindful and conscious decision to 'action something' and then practising to ingrain habits.

SLOW AND STEADY WINS THE RACE... OR THE ORGASM!

Now, depending on where you find yourself amongst all those questions and just how comfortable you are, will determine how you approach these next steps. Like our menopause, our self discovery experiences will be different. We all have varying relationships with our bodies, our sexuality and our 'ooh la la' moments. Try not to overthink the steps that Tania mindfully walked me through, which were: **what we say, what we see and how we touch.**

> *You have to make a choice to have this relationship, it's work, it's effort, it's daily. But's it's transformative, and the bi-product? A flow of healthy positive energy...flowing to every part of your being.*
>
> Tania Nishi

STEP 1. TALKING TO OURSELVES

Think about what you wrote before, the words you associate with your body and with this sacred part of you. To sack off the negatives, we need to re-learn and replace with words of self love and respect and it's a daily practise.

What are you going to call this part of you? Make a point of deciding here and now, even scribble it down if you wish:

Bringing this name and words of love in daily means associating them with either something specific, like affirmations, gratitude or meditation, and using your chosen name in the lingo where they should be spoken. For example, calling this part of you for what it is to your GP, Meno doctor, partner or children, whoever! Remember you're trying some things to endorse building respect for this part of yourself and rekindle the relationship.

Try actively giving this part of you some gratitude, it feels bizarre at first but words are powerful. For me, I thank her for being strong and resilient, for giving me pleasure and for the power that I'm learning to unleash through her. Sometimes this is out loud or sometimes written down.

What are you grateful to your [...] for?

Sometimes when I'm focused with intention or just when I'm in a moment of noticing. I will kind of cheer her on, big her up and think about my whole pelvic area expanding full of light and love.

I'm big on affirmations but had never connected them with any parts of my body specifically. Tania threw down what felt like a gauntlet of a challenge, for me not only to say these positive words, but to say them butt naked in front of a mirror! Tania believes this is the most powerful way to connect. I honestly squirmed at the idea and empathise with anyone who doesn't own a full length mirror. With Tania knowing full well my whole wardrobe door was a huge one... I couldn't exactly postpone the challenge. It felt totally awkward to just stand. Not pose or position myself to seem more flattering, just stand and speak to my body. I'm still finding my groove with this, not only with the affirmations, or the standing, but in truly feeling them all in the same moment...work in progress! Some of the things I say are:

"I'm going to get comfortable with saying Yoni."

"I'm on a journey to re-connecting to my Yoni."

"I hold love & light within & can let go of any anger I feel"

MY AFFIRMATIONS

Write your own here from the heart. Perhaps put them somewhere you can remind yourself. Remember, whilst you speak these words, to picture your relationship getting better.

★

☆

☆

Time to ask yourself, what fills you with more dread, touching or really looking at yourself? Once answered, go to the section and start there! For me it was touch...so I'm heading there first!

STEP 2. TOUCH – EXPLORE, EXPLORE, EXPLORE!

The association we have with touching ourselves or being touched is deeply personal, depending on previous experiences. For example, there's a certain place on me that if touched in just the wrong way, I'm transported back immediately to a place of trauma — feeling sick to the stomach and ready to say 'adios' to the passionate moment. We're quick to know where we usually experience pain or tenderness, our bodies and minds memorise it so helpfully. We're less established when it comes to knowing exactly what we like and just how far we can take our pleasure. Again, we're often conditioned to think that a quick orgasm via that protruding love button, our clitoris, is job done. Or we should be able to have and use all the copious toys on the market, not forgetting the sacred 'G spot', the holy grail. And don't even get me started on gushing and squirting ejaculation!

Tania again proposed that it's time to release ourselves from the conditioning and sack the pressure of all that off, because it all says more about society, marketing and money than truly understanding what pleasures you. For example, touching yourself might simply start by running your fingers over your torso or holding your hand over your vulva, stark naked or dressed like an Eskimo, it's by the by – how you feel comfortable is the main thing.

Reconnecting with touch – a daily practise!

- ✓ Set intentional time aside, even just a few minutes. With the sole purpose to feel pleasure
- ✓ Try not to get in your own way of the above!
- ✓ Take it as slow as you need to
- ✓ You don't have to go straight for the clit! Massaging, tickling or running hands or fingers over any part of your body that feels good, make the most of exploring
- ✓ When you're ready to go there, really feel around, there is no taboo, feel how sensations change
- ✓ Put down the toys, switch off the porn, using skin to skin for at least the first thirty days – even if you're a masturbating master!
- ✓ Use your vaginal moisturisers, lubes or ointments. It's ok to get jiggy putting them on
- ✓ You don't need to penetrate to have pleasure - fact!
- ✓ You don't have to be alone, bring in a partner or a trusted friend, expert or Yoni healer

How could you make this part of your daily routine?

How does this make you feel? Use this space to makes notes after your exploration time, describing the sensations felt and what was pleasurable or uncomfortable:

My Menopause, My Journal, My Rules!

List parts of your anatomy you know - take a moment to google and see if you missed any!

> We'll continue a bit more onto pleasurable touch and the big 'O' in a bit, but before we get too explosive and I lose you to a world of more positive moans and groans, it's time to check in, literally, as we explore another important factor... looking at ourselves!

STEP 3.
SEEING IS BELIEVING

Ok, so looking at one's folds was not so difficult for me. I mean I wasn't walking around with a hand mirror swinging between my thighs, but I had to take less of a deep breath than dealing with touch. This felt physical and intrusive, almost like at any point I could set off a memory bomb of trauma with just a wrongly placed stroke. With looking and *really* seeing I took the mindset that every other 'Tom, Dick and even Harry's sister's doctor' had looked in detail at my yoni, so maybe it was time I really understood what all the fuss was about! For you, looking at yourself might fill you with dread, generally admiring ourselves doesn't come easy, but it may be far deeper rooted than that. So, we're being brave here but be brave at your own pace.

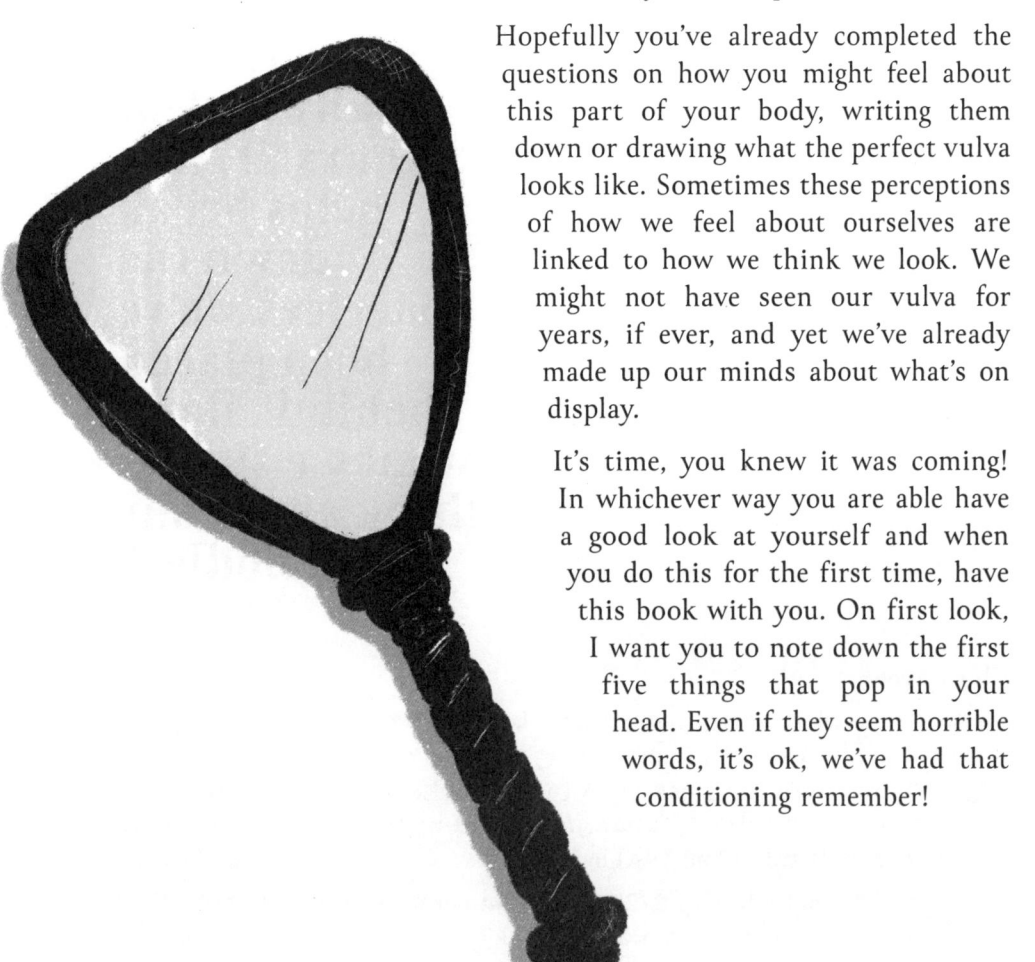

Hopefully you've already completed the questions on how you might feel about this part of your body, writing them down or drawing what the perfect vulva looks like. Sometimes these perceptions of how we feel about ourselves are linked to how we think we look. We might not have seen our vulva for years, if ever, and yet we've already made up our minds about what's on display.

It's time, you knew it was coming! In whichever way you are able have a good look at yourself and when you do this for the first time, have this book with you. On first look, I want you to note down the first five things that pop in your head. Even if they seem horrible words, it's ok, we've had that conditioning remember!

Write the first five things that come to mind positive or negative:

♛

♛

♛

♛

♛

> 'Like with touch,' Tania explained, 'it's important to make time to really look at yourself, this helps break down the barriers we've been placed behind; about what we should think about our own bodies'.

Think about:
Do you know what all the parts are? Can you name or see them all? Spend a while doing this, especially on your first go. Having a look regularly not only gets you used to seeing yourself in this way, it's also important for noticing changes from a health perspective which we'll touch on (pardon the pun) in a bit.

I would urge you to do this every now and then, or at least after your thirty days of re-discovery and ask that question of yourself again.

YOU'VE GOT SOME NERVE...

Let's chat communication. Not just between you and your own body, but how your body communicates with itself before you share with those around you, about what you like and don't like. We've touched on removing the pressure to find pleasure and there is no better analogy to use than that of the clitoris! This little bean that sits amongst the folds has often been the sole area of focus on how we get the 'Oooh yes yes yes train' out the station. Small but power punching it gets it fair share of focus. So, what if I told you that the clitoris has over 10,000 nerve endings and I'm not just talking about that bit we see! That little hooded berry is just the front really. It's the top of an underground world of pleasure, that's wired within your pelvic area... and its sole purpose? Pleasure! That's it...there's (in biological terms) no other purpose for it than lighting you the hell up! Pathways of nerves work like electrical currents, sparking, ready, and when you find the right connections? Boom! A light is ignited and your relationship to pleasure is well underway. Now what better act of wellness is there? Trouble is...it comes with an element of shame vs pressure.

Masterbation is meditation, it's one of your five a day!

TANIA NISHIV

PUTTING THE 'OH' IN ORGASMIC!

Clitoral, penetrative, multiple, G spot, O spot, get on top and rock spot... Oh, for goodness sake, do we really need to hit them *all* to have mind blowing sex? Or orgasm so hard it feels as if our bladders might burst? Again, let that belief go, because a lot of this is myth! With over half of woman having faked one, some not ever having had one, most cumming quicker alone than with a partner, the stats show we're still not fully connected with what it all means, so let's keep pleasure simple.

Just think about the beautiful map of nerves in the clitoris and how those nerves reach throughout your body. The G spot gland? The back of the clitoris! That particular place on your left labia – yep, the nerves from your clitoris. And why do I get that *oh so good* tingle in that spot on my lower groin? Ohhhhh I get it now! Now you'll already have a good idea from the previous activities that you may feel pleasure from a whole host of other places across your entire body: back of your neck, your nipples, the side of your arms. So instead of thinking *can I get the G spot*, simply understand your own map more. This will also help you communicate it easier with anyone you're choosing to have some fun with.

Remember, we are worthy of this, embrace it, because it is so good for our hormonal health.

Have you ever had an orgasm? Whether yes, no or maybe, what makes you think that?

Sometimes, you can get the feeling of missing out. This could be for those reasons we've looked at, physically, mentally or because of what we're fed socially. The wonderful thing is you have the power with exploration to have varied types of orgasm, in different layers, with different feelings. Explore, explore, explore. You might be reading this never having experienced the rush, you may have had your vagina removed, or have symptoms that cause a nightmare around the areas we've been told we must get the feels. It's your body and it's important to try and push past the stories we tell ourselves (because we will), finding areas that make you feel great through your own rules. They could be in the most surprising of places, but you won't know until you open up to the possibility that you deserve to be in tune with yourself in this way.

I really can say that with perseverance, patience with myself and constant communication with the husband, my pleasure scale, along with body acceptance and confidence, is growing so much more than I ever thought it would do. I feel empowered and am taking this as a huge win for menopause, so I urge you to keep going!

> **I'd love for women's sexuality, pleasure and self love to be part of the conversation at the dinner table, just like we'd chat about the gym or going for a walk.**
>
> **I hope that the generations to come become connected to themselves, not only in a biological, functional sense, but as part of their wellness and their pleasure.**
>
> The Naked Coach

Now we're a little more in tune with our body and understand its power and what it means to be healthy through energy, it's time to make the link to the physical symptoms we can often suffer from. By exploring, creating pleasure and practising, you can make a huge impact on preventing things like vaginal dryness and Atrophy often associated with menopause, or improving things before they get too far. Yep, you heard me... masturbating really is medicinal! It's time to talk biological pelvic health.

Find the beaut that is Tania on Instagram: @tanianishiv

PELVIC HEALTH

When Estrogen levels get lower we notice our skin starting to change, becoming thin, a bit wrinkly and sometimes dry too. The skin inside our vagina and our vulva does exactly the same. For some this is a slight discomfort and for others it can become unbearable! It starts with vaginal dryness, things get a bit itchy, a bit painful and sex might start to feel difficult. Imagine not being able to sit on your chair at work, let alone think about having a quickie, so it's best not to ignore! We've established that pleasure and understanding how your vagina and vulva feel can massively help prevent this from becoming debilitating; 1) because you're super aware of what's normal for you and 2) encouraging natural lubrication as much as possible can help keep the skin healthy and strong. Issues like UTIs to full on incontinence, are known about but so often aren't talked about. We're quicker to accept that we'll never bounce on a trampoline again or the Tena Lady becomes a staple on the shopping list. But it doesn't have to be that way.

I chatted to Kim Vopni, a Pelvic Physio Therapist and author, who is known as the Vagina Coach. Kim shared her knowledge with me and the things we need to be aware of.

Kim explained that we should start with our posture as we're often guarded in how we hold ourselves, meaning our pelvis sits in a particular way which can cause pain. We may have experienced prolapse, leaking, incontinence or things have moved around after surgery, all contributing to our pelvis being on guard. We then rush around day to day without giving posture a second thought, so it's good to slow down and notice what our own holding patterns are. Kim asked me: 'Are you tilting, tight or squeezing?' She told me how having good posture – where your hamstrings are lengthened and you're slightly clenched, keeping your diaphragm in alignment – is really important. Slower exercises like yoga, pilates or working with a pelvic physiotherapist help to focus strength in this area. No-one should have to take endless trips to the loo, wear pads in case you cough or laugh, forever, there are things you can do to help:

- ✓ Seek a referral to a pelvic physio
- ✓ Use pelvic toys called Kegel trainers (different to pleasure toys) which specifically strengthen the muscles within
- ✓ If you're more comfortable wearing something for leaks until you see improvement, check out eco-friendly underwear/swimwear. They're much comfier, better for the planet and look super nice

GET JUICY!

Kim really honed in on the point that when you start to notice things become less juicy or things feel irritable, like itching or discomfort, it's time to act.

I remember mentioning to a menopause specialist that I was rather dry as she mulled over my extremely low Estrogen levels on my blood results. In a rather well-to-do voice she responded, 'I'm not surprised dear, you need to give your vagina some love and get some Estrogen up there! I'll prescribe you some moisturisers and pessaries'. I literally laughed out loud down the phone, but realised we are entitled to this stuff!

Kim reassured me that this was all a great place to start and we chatted about how we're so comfortable to moisturise our face and bodies with all manner of things and yet we should remember:

same skin, different body part, simple!

ATROPHY

This is where that initial dryness is left untreated and the skin alters becoming really thin and almost like glass. It can split, becoming unhealthy where it should be plump and strong. Kim got me to think about the wall of my vagina being like a pleated skirt. As Estrogen drops this not only thins but becomes tighter, more like a pencil skirt slowly narrowing down. So, we need to make things supple, stretchy and lubed up again. Warning signs are:

- Burning
- Itching
- Pain during or after sex
- Discharge changes
- Not getting wet, despite feeling the feels
- Frequent Urinary Tract Infections
- Pain when you pee
- Needing the loo more
- Needing to pee quickly

It can be common because often we don't feel comfortable to address things early. Once Atrophy has taken hold it's a symptom that, unfortunately, you don't really grow out of, meaning this could stay with you into post-menopause. Fear not, there are things that you can do to help and I'd highly recommend you look out for and go read some specific books/blogs or watch some videos, making notes in here, of course! So, we can get through a day without always looking for where the loo is or exercise becoming the enemy, we need to swiftly tackle our parched pussies. Because mixing Atrophy with a drop in sexual desire, low confidence or moods, we've got the danger of 007 with a cocktail recipe for dry – without the Martini.

Look after your LIPS!

WHAT CAN HELP?

- ✓ Go to the doctor. Just do it! Head over to Rule 4 for a reminder on walking in there like you've got this! Be clear on your symptoms and whether this is your vagina or your vulva? And be prepared for the white glove to come out!

- ✓ Only wash with water! Soap strips away moisture and disrupts the PH balance. This goes for soaps that claim to be for our nether regions too.

- ✓ Get acquainted with intimate moisturisers or lubes, even if you haven't noticed any dryness, to keep things supple! Check ingredients, opting for specific brands that are made for this purpose (not sex), as others can trigger PH changes. Water-based and those with hydrochloric acid retain moisture and heal the tissue.

- ✓ There are creams, lubes, ointments and pessaries to moisten and dilators and doughnuts to promote flexibility. Like all of this, it'll be test and investment of your time, until you find what works. You may also want to ask for vaginal Estrogen as a preventative to stop things worsening.

Atrophy is also the last calling card before leading to a more serious diagnosis for things like Lichens disease and even cancers, so Kim stressed again how important it is to start tuning in and not shy away from including your pelvic area into your daily skincare routine. Getting connected and (where you can) pleasuring yourself regularly, will all help keep things healthy.

In this world of social media, we're inundated with transformation. Wouldn't it be awesome if it didn't have to be - transform? Because we'd have informed choices and body knowledge around pelvic health, throughout all its stages. We'd all feel comfortable and empowered and prevention would thrive.

Kim Vopni – The Vagina Coach

Kim Vopni can be found on Instagram @vaginacoach or www.vaginacoach.com

Note down anything you feel you need to here:

INTERVAL OF EVENTS

Back and forth we go again between GP, receptionist and the Meno doc, finally getting to the point of hearing the receptionist's glorious words, 'yep we can get you fitted with an implant locally at the surgery. Ring Monday'. I'm elated...this is it...here comes the game-changing little thing of magic.

Monday: Anna sighs as she says, 'Sorry, no, we don't do it here, you need a GP referral back to a gynea, it's possibly a ten week wait and we're not sure they even do them geographically in this area'.

'ARE YOU FUCKING KIDDING ME!' I scream on mute. 'I really liked you Anna, but I'm afraid you're off the Christmas card list!' I'm crying, proper snotty tears.

Oh, there's more. I know I'm exhausted too. My phone pings with a text from the surgery, yep, a text, like some feeble break up to confirm that alas, it iS true: no hospitals in mine or surrounding areas offer this service. I'm looking at the screen caught in a postcode lottery, like what now? This was like sending a text to a diabetic saying, 'Sorry mate, you're not going to get your insulin. Good luck!' What utter bollocks.

So, my choices: 1) Wait months to head to a far away clinic with so little Estrogen in my body that I'm literally exhausted and forgetting how to finish typing this sentencccceeeee. 2) Travel six miles up the road (yep just six), have the implant fitted within two weeks (you read correctly) by going private – for a hefty £500. I've booked the appointment and my kidney is currently for sale on eBay!

This is the situation until the medical world catches up with the fact that menopause isn't going anywhere, and we'll have to keep fighting the fight and advocating for ourselves. I shared with you that as my Estrogen drained, I lost my shizzle so badly I didn't want to live. I didn't know what was happening to me then, thank goodness I do now.

Knowledge is, of course, power. It helps us understand 'why?' I know that however tough it feels right now and however dark, there is light. Even if I have to wait a little while longer than hoped. I know that what is happening to me is a hormonal thing, not because I'm a crappy person. We need to stand up for ourselves, be relentless in not giving up for our own beautiful bodies and minds that are carrying our souls through the next part of our life. Second spring or the reign of the Queen-hood... We owe ourselves the love and compassion to keep keeping on.

Rule 7   Start A Re-Vulva-Lution

you won't fall forever

you won't fall forever

RULE 8
Soothe Your Messy Mind

LOSING MYSELF

A few years back I was on a mental spiral, my confidence suddenly vanished, I could not find the joy in anything. I was angry yet numb and I felt like my life was fake with no purpose as I crept slowly and silently into a breakdown. I hadn't realised how much my relationships were strained, losing the plot at work as paranoia took its grasp and negative thoughts would chatter, disrupting my clarity.

Driving the kids to school one morning the radio sang yet I couldn't hear the melody, and as the low November morning sun shone into my eyes, I just didn't want to squint to see the road. I no longer wanted to press the brakes to save us.

The Boy bellowed something from the back, the dark was disrupted, and I pressed foot to pedal, slowing us in time. Hazily, I dropped the kids off, drove home and picked up the phone to a helpline. This was just over two years after my hysterectomy...and this was the start of me truly starting to heal. After two of the hardest hours, I was swiftly booked in with a therapist for Cognitive Behavioural Therapy (CBT). A few days later, once at the doctors, I was offered anti-depressants and formally diagnosed with depression. With a fear of feeling worse on the meds, I chose not to cash in the prescription, thinking I'd just need a few weeks rest. I did not return to work for six months after that day.

I chatted twenty-two times with Dr John and it was, in fact, he who connected the dots that this – although it ticked all the boxes of a mental illness – was significantly related to me being in surgical menopause. He nudged the right questions and as time and healing went on, I would learn through our talks and my own research, just how affected I'd been both physically and mentally from endless surgeries, my lack of care post-hysterectomy and the effects of being hormone deficient.

My mental health was, and still is, a ride, and I can now see clearly how it is linked not only to the physical changes that menopause puts us through but also how biologically things shift in our brains. How past trauma or buried feelings may surface and how perfectly okay it is to seek help, alongside finding tools that can help us manage when it might feel rough. I really wouldn't be writing this if I hadn't fully spilled my deepest thoughts on the table that day. If I hadn't taken the advice of a friend who once said, 'if you ever have talking therapy, just don't hold back, let it all go because you have nothing to lose except yourself'.

I'm passing that advice straight onto you, along with a few things that might help you navigate some of the symptoms that affect what we think our minds are telling us and those times when we want to throw a hammer at a face, or you need a proper snotty cry. If something isn't working for you, change it!

Sometimes our bodies and minds connect, going haywire, and this is usually a sign to slow the fuck down. When you feel like you've lost yourself a bit, think about what your frustrations are. What could you do to change them? What expectations on you are your own, and which are from others? Sometimes we have these little noggins (I love that word) of mental disruption on our path to trip us up.

But it's important to know that with all the things that drive us mad, cause pain or make us go grrrr, they are being done for us, not to us. There is always something to learn from the chaos, however difficult it feels. I have learnt that writing my own rules around my mental health is just as important, if not more important, than filling my body with HRT, medications or supplements. Because in the times when those things aren't available or working, this is the stuff that keeps me afloat. So, I'm sharing the serious action and the not so serious too, because there's always a need for light and shade amongst the mess of our minds.

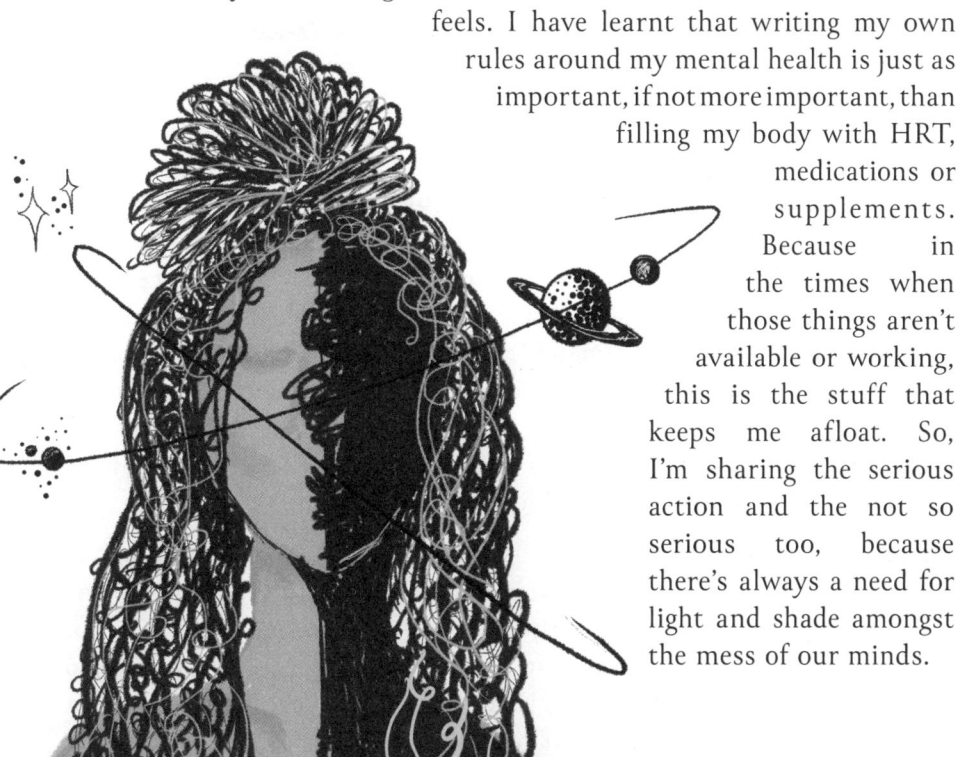

> ## IMPORTANT NOTE
>
> Mental illness and mental health are two different things. Our general mental health ebbs and flows, which is normal, we can all expect good and bad times and equip ourselves with tools and knowledge that can help get us through.
>
> Mental illness is a whole different book. It's multi-faceted and complicated, which is where professionals and medications step in, specific for each individual's requirements.
>
> If you find you are feeling lost, or that you are so low and depressed these words are a bleurgh, I really urge you to make a call, starting with one word… 'Help'.
>
> Know that you deserve that. Helplines are there waiting for you at the back, you are loved and you are not alone.

STRESS

We're starting here because stress is often the root of where our mental state manifests and what's not helpful is there's no real medical definition for it. I guess that's because it's so personal to the individual. Since we've walked the earth our brains' flight or fight alarm has bellowed, releasing Adrenalin and Cortisol, ultimately aimed to protect us from danger in the same way as our ancestors. Back then they had to decide whether to fight the Sabre Tooth or shit their loin cloths and run! But us, we're faced with over-stimulated situations or pressures and although our dangers have changed, this stress trigger kicks off in much the same way.

We all need *some* stress to help us make decisions and assess danger and without any at all we just wouldn't survive. The type that lingers between burnout and boredom…that sweet spot of feeling like you've got it all together, being productive and having all the energy, that's the good stuff. Rather than balance or striving for 'stress free', it's more about harmony and understanding your own sweet spot. We can't eliminate it and when stress increases beyond our own manageable capacity, it takes its toll on our bodies and mind. From bloating or painful flare ups to our legs giving way leaving us in a heap on the floor. And stress is the common underlying factor that fuels rage, anxiety, panic attacks and even depression.

Everyone manages stress differently and we find some days we're coping, others days not so much, so working out what is stressing you out can be a good place to start. You can then look for ways to decrease those triggers and learn how to manage the things that have to stick around.

This is the life skill we don't get taught and we definitely need to be practising, especially when our fuse may be just that little bit shorter! It was the stupid small stuff that broke me to burnout, a concoction of washing on the landing, the expectation of family dinners, ping pinging of emails and chasing all those HRT appointments! Along with my few suggestions, there are huge amounts of stress reducing ideas out there. It's a good time to find your rules that work. But essentially, unless we make the link to self, check in, rest and communicate what we need to others, we're going in circles. **It will take action and it's going to have to come from you.**

The Stress Sweet Spot
Loosely based on Posen & Nixon theory

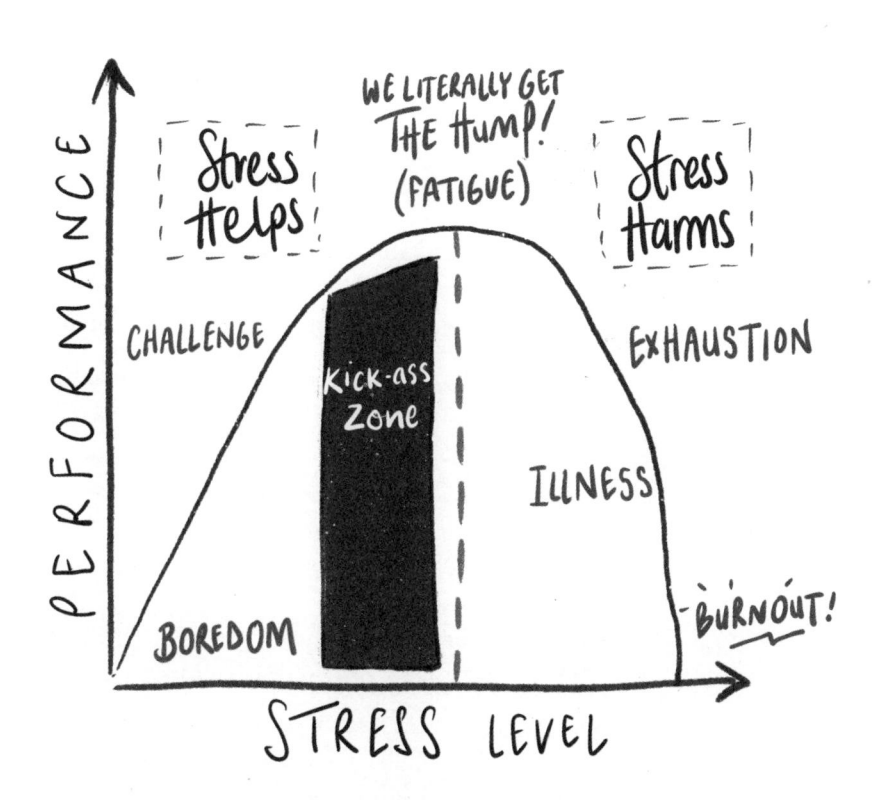

PERFORMANCE

Stress Helps

WE LITERALLY GET THE HUMP! (FATIGUE)

Stress Harms

CHALLENGE

Kick-ass Zone

EXHAUSTION

ILLNESS

BOREDOM

BURNOUT!

STRESS LEVEL

Rule 8   Soothe Your Messy Mind

OVERWHELM

Alongside stress, overwhelm is something that creeps up and suddenly everything just feels too much. It can be one thing or feeling, maybe the guilt of not being the person you once were, or that you just don't want to be around your partner right now. Or it could be multiple things happening at once and your coping mechanisms grind, leaving things feeling out of control. These are many of the factors we'll cover that can play into overwhelm and we'll look at how you can take back some control, by building your own toolkit from things I've tried. Writing your own rules by trying some new stuff of your own. Remember, overwhelm is something we experience whether in menopause or not, so it's okay to acknowledge and tell someone from the off that you're feeling overwhelmed and need to slow down and re-focus.

What are the main things that are stressing you out right now?

Rule 8   Soothe Your Messy Mind

Be mindful about your capacity

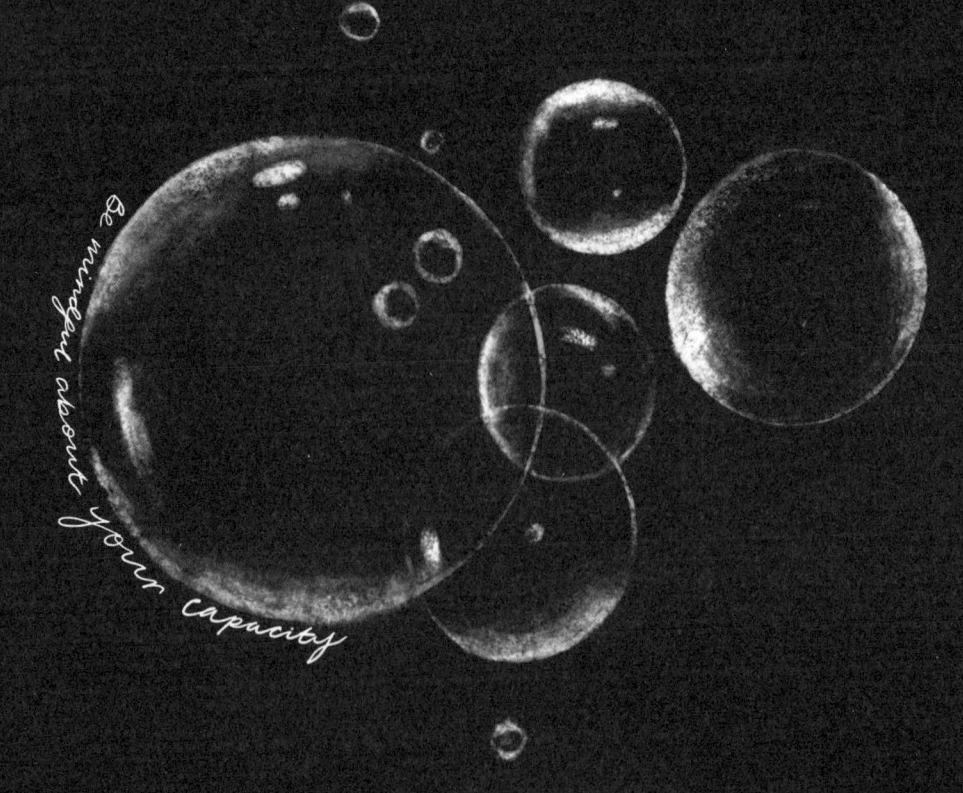

LESS OF THE 'YES', LESS OF THE STRESS

Do you remember that time in Covid when we had 'bubbles'? Where we could only connect or be in contact with a certain amount of people? Weird times, right? It's time to look at your own bubble. I used to be a total 'yes person' but the capacity in my bubble became over stretched. It had no more space for air and simply went pop! Emerging from lockdown at the same time as emerging from my breakdown, I thought very carefully about who and what I would invite into my bubble.

Being a 'yes' person is giving all your energy to everyone else; friends, family, being the planner, the doer, the one who makes everyone laugh or organises the events, blah blah blah. It's okay to reserve some energy and say 'no,' especially if it isn't serving you right now. It's important to clarify that 'no' isn't the same as 'maybe...let me check the diary' or even 'sounds good', only to cancel later. Complaining all week about the thing you're squeezing into your already busy schedule or spending far too much worry power thinking of copious excuses to get out of what you didn't want to do in the first place is a waste of your time and energy; just say 'no'. This will become easier for you with time and is surprisingly better for everyone involved. The outcome is that everyone is clear!

I get you. You're like, 'yeah ok...you haven't met my boss/mother/mate.' We all have those people that it seems are just too hard to avoid or turn down. The thing is these are exactly the people we have to say the word to first! If you say it in the right way, with an explanation, then you'll be surprised how those that love us or have our back at work are actually ok with it. In fact, they'd rather us be happy and less stressed; ultimately it allows them to re-plan from the off. People are not going to hate you for saying 'no' – simple! Explaining to my family that I just couldn't arrange the birthday collections at the moment or that they really needed to take charge of the table booking, because it really wasn't helping me navigate my mental health and brain fog, went down like a sack of... alright. I mean seriously it was okay! Sharing honestly with my mates that I didn't feel like the dinner out, or that the busy pub was making my anxiety worse, I just reassured them saying, 'so let's do something when I'm feeling I can give you my full attention' and they were fine...I kid you not! In fact, it helped open up conversations about feelings, mental health and this menopause stuff much more.

SAYING 'NO' IS SAYING 'YES' TO YOURSELF

Rule 8   Soothe Your Messy Mind

Make a list of things you need to say 'No' to more:

WHEN TO SAY 'HELL YEAH!'

Hurrah, 'yes' is not off the table completely. It's all about balancing choices that will serve you and in turn means that you can be fully there and present for everyone else. By saying 'no' to the stuff that zaps your energy, you make space for new opportunities and times where you *can* say 'yes', challenging yourself to try things that you might usually shy away from. We'll cover confidence later (we know this takes a knock in menopause), but did you know trying something new helps to increase confidence? When we start showing up to new things in our life, we're learning new confidence. It doesn't matter if you totally smash it, finding something you love, or if it turns into a huge 'dickhead moment' (I have these often). It all helps to build the next version of your kick-ass self! It's about reflecting on the act of saying 'yes' and not the outcome. The fact that you even went there is enough, anything else is a bonus or a learn. But remember, there is no room for the stuff we want to bring in or try unless we make space by saying 'no' first.

If you have a moment where you suddenly think 'oh look at me, I said yes outside my comfort zone', write it here as a reminder. Or challenge yourself if it stays empty:

Rule 8   Soothe Your Messy Mind

THE ART OF DELEGATION

I remember giving a list of all the stuff I do around the house to the hubs. Like all of it and asked to chat it over. His reply was 'Fuck off!' I obviously caught him on a bad day, but within ten minutes I'd planned our divorce, how we would co-parent and who would have the dog...me of course. After I cooled down, I realised divorce was an effort, so opted to give the conversation another go. I gently pushed the paper covered in jobs across the table and calmly stated, 'Currently I do all of these, so I don't mind which ones you choose to do, but you can take half.' I just stared at him, watching as he took off the list to make his choices...and he did!

Now, his consistency is questionable, and yes, the kids eat Tuna Pasta Bake every time he cooks, but I had to learn to keep quiet and we're further along than we were. It's definitely relieved some pressure I was feeling to do all the things.

What are some things you could share or ask someone else to do right now?

-
-
-
-
-
-

CREATING JOY!

Think of yourself as a balloon; every time something stressful comes along, water is added. The more stress, the more water, the balloon edging ever closer to capacity. Too much stress and it'll burst. What you need is a valve. So, when things get tight you can release the valve, letting the water trickle and the pressure reduce. **This valve is joy, and it works by you adding things into your life that bring you that joy.** I can't tell you what will bring you joy, which is why de-stressing ourselves is a personal thing. For me it's seeing friends, being playful or writing. If you're struggling to think about what brings you joy, I'd like you to:

Write down all the things you loved doing as a child below:

Rule 8   Soothe Your Messy Mind

Now ask yourself, is there anything there that you can bring into your life now? Write them down and look into how you are going to do them, because this is the stuff you need to say, 'yes' to. You'll need to revisit this list when we talk confidence later:

JOY

Pushing ourselves to bring in the joy, counter-balancing the negatives and stretching a little out of our comfort zone can help us build new confidence. **Trying something completely different, even a little weird, is fun in itself.** Even if you never do it again you're gaining confidence in trying new things. This is something I did…

There isn't a single person who doesn't enjoy or need a good belly laugh, but what happens when you force yourself to do so? At a point where my confidence was low and stress at burnout needing to find the happiness, I discovered 'laughter yoga'. No downward dog required, and I did it from my front room. I was taken through a series of laughs, from 'hee hees' in the throat, moving to more nasal chuckles, to full on 'Bahahahahaha' belly benders. It felt quite bizarre at first, feeling like a right pleb, but before I knew it I was howling uncontrollably as the 'Laughter Man' kept things moving along, changing sounds for me to copy as I tried to hold the wee in! I experimented with laughter yoga one to one and also in a virtual group, where we'd start the day with just fifteen minutes of pure silliness. Hearing others was infectious, finding stomach muscles I'd not used in a while and oh my goodness did it feel great.

I'd recommend it to anyone, whether virtually or in person, because blimey, things can get so serious at times; sometimes we've got to belly laugh until our pelvic floors just can't take it! It will feel odd and unnatural but keep going. Because after just five to ten minutes of chuckles you'll leave feeling full of joy and mentally much better.

My Menopause, My Journal, My Rules!

My ideas of things to bring me *joy*

Rule 8 Soothe Your Messy Mind

Behind the Curtains

Heavy head the curtains pulled,
No work again today,
Tired on tired, lethargy looming,
Nothing useful to say.
Pull the duvet round myself,
Couldn't get up if I tried,
Full of angst, I'm so confused,
So many tears to be cried.

I cannot face the world outside,
My room will have to do,
I'm crying, dying, deep inside,
No one has a clue.
Motivation, fatigue, anxiety,
I've lost my get up and go.
Depression, darkness, deep despair
Where the fuck's my damn mojo?

Fitful sleep and moodswings,
Forgetting, feeling cross,
Never ending migraines
Is what I tell my boss.
Time off work so helpful,
My GP not so much,
Antidepressants offered,
If I want a crutch.

I'm 43, feel washed up,
Wrung out old and grey,
I need to get a grip on this,
Live life another day.
Who will I talk with,
About this fug of mine?
I used to be so happy, full of joy,
Do I now settle, just feeling 'fine'.

The lust I once felt has left me,
I fear it's never coming back,
Anyone dares to talk to me,
First line defence; attack.
My mind it's in a muddle,
My head always a spin,
I hate this bloody feeling,
How long now has it been?

I feel so blue, so desperate,
The black dog may appear,
I need, I want, to help myself,
There must be others near…
Get out, do something different,
So hard to take the leap,
If I don't do something drastic
I'll end up a mess, a heap.

Slowly the curtains open,
Light through the window appears,
Silently inside,
I cry some happy tears.
The open door gets closer,
Move towards it every day,
Perhaps I'll be able to articulate
What I really want to say.

Through the fog I see it,
It's still so far away,
Slowly, slowly catchy monkey,
I'll reach it come what may.
A hand extends to greet me,
It feels warm, envelops mine,
Brings me closer to its heart,
I know I will be fine.

This warmth I feel is my sisters,
My tribe, my menoflock.
A band of women suffering,
Some need support
around the clock.
A community I will build up,
A safe and open space,
A time, a place, a person,
To be that friendly face.

Menopause Mentoring,
Menopause friendly walks,
Monthly Menopause Cafe events,
Education, workshops, talks.
Midlife menopause coaching,
Recycling army stock,
Creating a menopause uniform,
Armed to rock with MenoFlock.

Confident to defend myself,
Knowledge I have devoured,
Reading, learning, listening,
I'm now educated, empowered.
Clearer head the curtains pulled,
I'm off to work today,
Energy, vigour, an action plan,
I have so much more to say.

**Written by
Gayle Stevens-White,
who started peri-
menopause at age
forty-one xxx**

**Gayle is a kickass
menopause activist
and coach, with a cool
clothing brand.**

Website: menoflock.com
Instagram: @gswmenoflock
& @rockandrebellion

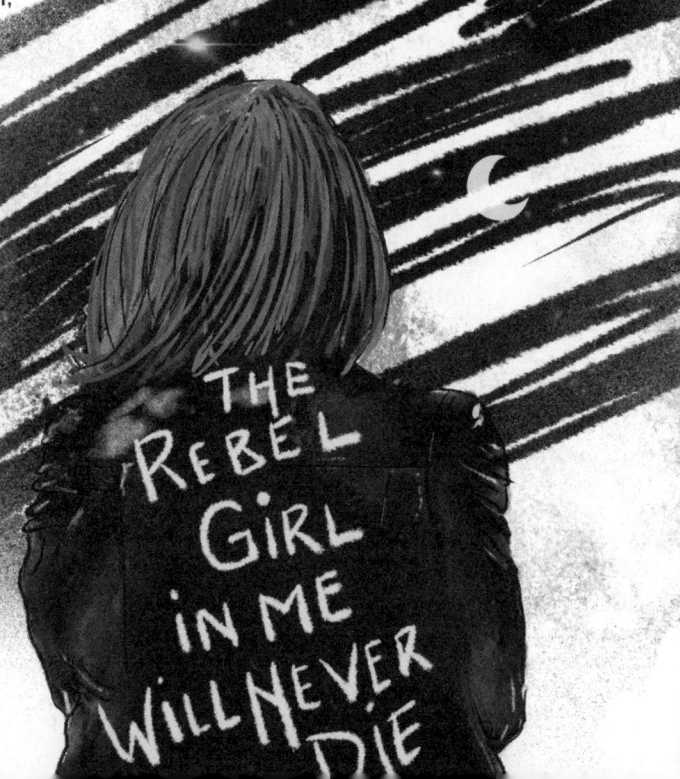

WE'RE ALL JUST DOING OUR BEST.

HORMONES IN THE HOUSE!

Can we just acknowledge for a second how bloody difficult it is to have the whirlwind of hormones in the house when you're dealing with your own fluctuating hormones, alongside toddler tantrums to pubescent tweens, and then there's the teenage years! Wow it's like watching penalties in an England final...who will come out on top? Who will be saved and who will be crushed to death for missing the net? I have absolutely zero advice in this department, other than acknowledging that there are days when I can cope, putting into practise all the tools shared and it's, menopause 1, puberty 0. And then there are the days when I just cry and say, 'fuck'...a lot!

RAGE!!!!

I'm talking where mild anger turns to blood boiling, seething, emotions and you absolutely lose your shit – hello rage! I feel huge guilt over this symptom as those that get the worst of me are mostly my husband and kids. There's often no explanation as to what triggers it and at its worst, it was over the petty stupid things!

Give me a drunk teen, a stupid life mistake or the school ringing to say The Boy has been a bit of a dick and I can handle the embarrassment, the chats, the controlled tempered response in a fairly reflective way. Leave crumbs all over the kitchen side or the tornado of washing that seems to just fall off them onto the stairs, landing, anywhere – as if they've flamboyantly stripped on purpose leaving a trail of mess – then, at my worst, I've lost it. The hoover has been thrown across a room, I've smashed Lego that's taken hours to build and un-done all the years of hard work to not swear in front of the kids, by screaming 'FOR FUCK'S SAKE' so loud that Janice at No 24 would flinch and the dog scuppers off to hide!

It's not pretty. I'm not proud of these moments and, of course, afterwards I apologise, talk it through and have worked hard to try and manage this part of me that erupts. One of the first things I did was try to learn my triggers, dealing with them by putting them top of the list. For example, I set a new rule – if it doesn't hit the wash bin, it doesn't get washed. Now I still pick up the clothes sprawled around the house, but they get thrown straight back into the kids' rooms. It took a few hairy moments of no clean school shirts, but I continued to have a word with myself, take a breath and realise that them learning was more effective than my fucks being given in a huge rage!

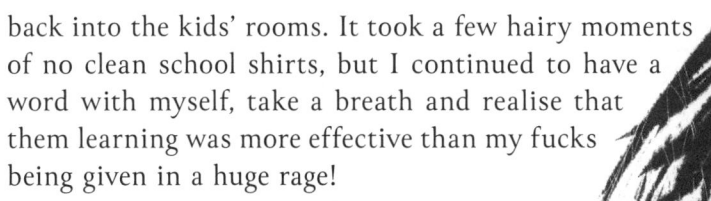

IT'S OK NOT TO HAVE YOUR SHIT TOGETHER

Sometimes we do just want to screeeeeaaaaaammmm and it can be therapeutic when done in a room on your own or in the car, music blaring! However, there are also those thoughts we have that we daren't say out loud...come on we all have them? Those thoughts that, if they reached the government on some telepathic search engine, we'd be locked up. The ones that we could never take back if we said them out loud. So, I'm giving you permission to release them.

When you need to, **turn to the back of this book and you'll find some pages called 'Scream on a Page'.**

This is your space to write, draw, scribble, whatever it is that you need to say and get out of yourself. Once you're done, rip it out and rip it up...yes really! Burn or bin it (somewhere never to be found by others) and let that purge of rage be released.

There is no need to keep it in the book...it is not serving you.

there's zero shame

Rule 8   Soothe Your Messy Mind

However, when shit's gone down and certain people have just got on the final nerve I have left, I've fantasised, pondering if I could bump them off in one of the ways below and get away with it!

- Put them on the phone to your GP's receptionist for menopause advice and support - death by frustration.

- Put your chin hairs in their pasta - At least you'll be smooth for their funeral!

- The 'did you really just suggest that while I'm so hormonal' death stare, holding for approximately thirty-three seconds - Boom!

- HRT patches (only really effective with larger brands) placed neatly over where you might find hot air...you know where I'm going with this!

- Blowing them into the next county with your raging screams, preferably to someone else who can cook for them!

- Get them dressed up for a night out and then stick them in a sauna on high...hot flush anyone?

- There are approximately forty-one ways you can bump someone off with a banana and some of them you get to eat it first - potassium is found in bananas and potassium is much needed in menopause...win win!

- Start a conversation with 'So my vulva and vagina are so irritable and dry right now...' - they literally die with embarrassment, easy!

- That herbal tea you're drinking to relieve symptoms - let them try it... with cyanide!

- Suffocation by saggy boob - only one needed.

CONFIDENCE BOOST

Lack of Estrogen and even Testosterone can affect our confidence levels, or lower our self-esteem and when we go through change it can knock us sideways, leaving us questioning ourselves. **Losing confidence is disconnecting from the trust we hold in our ability.** My confidence took a massive hit; I'd always been the one to chat with anyone, travel alone, speak up in meetings or talk to a huge audience on stage, it just didn't bother me. Yet suddenly I'd lost my voice, I didn't believe in myself anymore.

Self esteem is different, it's the emotional value we put upon our worth. When this is low we're more likely to fear rejection, are less resilient to failure, don't respect ourselves and lean on crutches like alcohol or food. We create an inner critic.

It's possible to have both together or to be super confident and yet have low self esteem. Hence, why a musician may crush a performance, then in private fill a void with drugs. The way to re-build either of these is by getting to know yourself again and re-programme your thinking. It's more than hormones!

No-one is born more or less confident than the person next to them. It's not genetic, nor is it a gift, a talent or just how you are...it's learnt. Practising something repeatedly, then believing our own success within, over time gives us a boost! Our own belief is an important point here, because even when we get validation from others we have to truly feel the success ourselves to gain confidence, and your version of success will be different to mine. Growing up, our environment, circumstances at home and those we have around us, all add to our confidence bucket too and it's the same now. So what I'm saying is all is not lost, we just need to re-learn.

I was introduced to a concept called the confidence buckets by Lucienne Shakir a fierce female empowerment coach and still find it hugely helpful, so I'm sharing it for you to try.

Think about the things you used to love doing as a child, say around age 7-11, maybe re-visit that list you made earlier, you'll need it next!

THE CONFIDENCE BUCKETS

These two buckets represent full of confidence and one lacking and empty. In the full bucket, list five things you did as a child that you felt confident in or loved (mine would be: creating, exploring, social settings, etc.). Then, in the empty one, list five things that you're struggling in confidence with now (mine: feeling the need to impress, not knowing the information I need, needing to be perfect, etc.).

If you need more than five things in your buckets go for it; scribble all over the page.

Rule 8   Soothe Your Messy Mind

SO WHERE AM I GOING WITH THIS?

I used to love exploring and by the age of ten I'd be out alone on my bike for hours, imagining great expeditions. Yes, I was encouraged by my parents, given freedom, time and a bike. But I would do this often, practising routes, learning when I went off track, making my way through an adventure and home again for dinner, all unknowingly building an inner belief of success.

I was secure making friends too. Parties didn't phase me, the first to chat, or find a common connection and always wanted to be the one to get up on stage. This may have been verbalised by those around me…'she's a confident talker, or always doing a show,' but it was in those inner moments as child that I felt proud – that's success, belief and confidence teaming up. Think about how many times you got to practise the things in your full bucket, how many times did you truly feel successful yourself?

Whereas my empty bucket houses feelings like – I always need to impress or I'm the one with less of a voice competing with my brothers. Then menopause hit and it seemed to dent the armour of my confidence bucket too. This hammered my self-esteem, to where I didn't feel I belonged. I became quiet, even feeling I was a bad person. This was the story I told myself until recently. However, now we know confidence is learnt and linked to our own feelings of success, you can work on building back up, not only things you may have lost confidence in recently but even things you didn't feel confident in before menopause. There are a few ways to do this, but it starts with flipping the switch on mindset.

Self Acceptance
– Acknowledging and accepting what is making your confidence or self esteem feel rubbish right now.

Ask yourself, is this serving me or not?
– There may be things in your empty bucket as a direct result of situations you have been in or people you have been around. Asking yourself this allows you to see if this is even an area you want to work on? This can feel tough if the answer is no. Sometimes it means letting go of people or situations and that may feel painful...at first!

Switch the lingo
– This is challenging your inner critic, allowing yourself to say, 'actually I am good at....' Or giving yourself permission to love and value yourself more with positive self talk, closing down negative patterns. Surrounding yourself with positive influence helps. Think about the people you hang out with the most, do they inspire you to fill your cup?

The art here is to use what's in your confidence bucket to top up the empty. You can do this by connecting areas that are similar and writing out some statements...like writing your own rules to your confidence levels.

For example:

> I know I'm good in social settings, so I don't have to feel like I need to impress
>
> I'm great at exploring, so I can be great at finding out the information or resources I need to help me
>
> I'm creative and authentic so I don't need to appear perfect

Have a go at writing your own statements using what you've put in your buckets (reminding yourself of these statements helps you rebuild confidence and when you're trying something new):

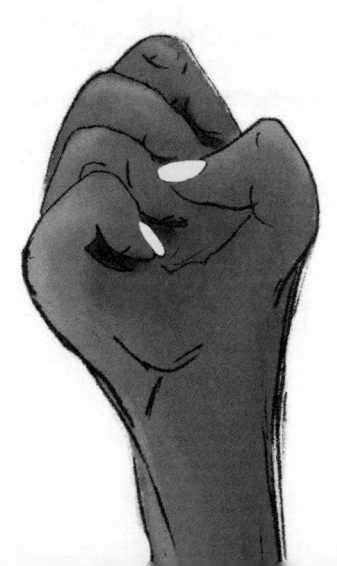

♛

♛

♛

♛

♛

♛

♛

♛

♛

Your statements, alongside focusing on positive self worth, things like accepting compliments or saying No assertively, will reset the confidence foundations. Growing our self-esteem, by trying new things or bringing in that joy we talked about whist continuing to do the things you're already badass in (feeling that success), really does work.

I felt this when I returned back to work after that six months off, I would think: I just can't speak to people like I used to. How on earth would I ever get back to training or delivering something on stage? So, I just focused on one small thing at a time. My first job: chat with a few colleagues a week, that was all. Slowly I put myself into situations where I needed to speak, like meetings and forums. Talking about things I was passionate about made it easier. I would voice record my ideas or blogs and eventually started a podcast so I got used to hearing my voice out loud again. I spoke on socials through stories and lives and I said 'yes' when asked to deliver virtual talks, always re-visiting my statement, 'I'm creative and authentic, so I don't need to be perfect'. Eventually I built myself back up to now, a loud mouth shouting about something I truly believe in and ready to jump on stage and tell the world about my menopause!

You really can do this too when you let the things you are confident in spill over to nurture whatever's worthy of your energy in your empty bucket – then watch your confidence grow.

NAVIGATING THROUGH BRAIN FOG!

"I thought I was losing my mind."

I cannot tell you how many times I have said or heard this phrase from those experiencing menopause. So, let me reassure you...nope you're not going mad, despite the feeling that marshmallows are growing in your head, competing for a 'fluffy bunny' contest. You simply have hormones fluctuating or zapped altogether and your Estrogen is playing silly – it's one of the main hormones our brain needs. Our language skills, attention, mood and memory are just a few of the things Estrogen gives us to function and hold it together. It's no big surprise that brain fog is one of the symptoms that we find the most difficult, despite the myth that it's hot flushes!

There is research happening on the effects so have a good read of the latest findings if you wish. For now, let's explore what eases this common blurriness of thinking and shed light on what could be making things worse.

Brain fog feels pretty grim, like you're not the person you thought you were. I've had women confide in me they thought they had early dementia! Misplacing the small to the big, to the really important stuff, is not only annoying for you, but equally for those around you who might be thinking, 'what on earth is going on?'

It's a real struggle so try to communicate and understand what it feels like for you *all*. This in itself relieves the pressure of feeling like you have to hide. You never know…your teenager may empathise (pffff) or you might get help with the laundry because you've forgotten how to work the machine!

I'm a brain fog pro, let me tell you as I sit here in my brother's quiet country cottage, inking this section in peace, less than two hours ago I was in the middle of one of those not-so-road-like lanes in the emptiness of nowhere. Completely off track, with the wrong village in my head, I felt totally muddled, well and truly lost and anxious. Its name just wouldn't come into my memory. I called my Dad to remind me where I was heading. To clarify, my bro lives fourteen miles from my house and I've been there numerous times, how bloody stupid did I feel?

Top tip: Go nowhere without your phone, a sat nav, an in-car picnic and some toilet roll.

Severe brain fog showed up for me at work too. I couldn't function. Memory lapses became severe, and I felt like I was unable to tackle multiple tasks let alone learn new things. I'd always been such a quick learner and fast paced…it felt debilitating. I spoke openly about it, tried to do one thing at a time within capacity, but eventually it got me and I took some time away from work again to rest my mind. This was while I awaited my implant and my Estrogen was extremely low. I had to learn patience, hoping that one day I would be able to do all the things again. It took me a while to get over the guilt and shame of being off again, but I knew the tools I had learnt from before had to kick in. This was the only way I could manage myself, be a Mum and reconnect once more to those things that come before the job. I had to put my own rules into action.

I also struggle with:

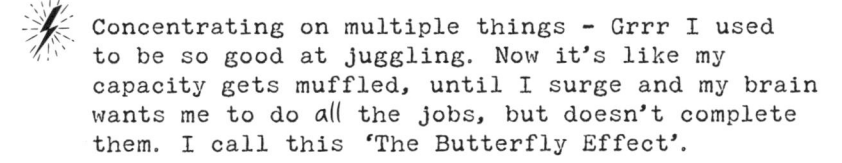

- Concentrating on multiple things – Grrr I used to be so good at juggling. Now it's like my capacity gets muffled, until I surge and my brain wants me to do all the jobs, but doesn't complete them. I call this 'The Butterfly Effect'.

- Remembering words, misplacing names of things, places or people. I once forgot my friend's name… she has the same name as me for goodness sake!

- Absorbing conversations/instructions and (if no notes made)…yep it's gone! I have to use all my brain power to zone in, constantly hearing from the husband or kids…'I told you that!'

- Finding the car! If I could have built some way to safely park inside this book, I would have.

- Putting things in my calendar, reading them, then still forgetting to do the thing. School trips, missed appointments, happy belated birthday anyone?

- Paying bills, yikes!

- Constantly forgetting that the chocolate fell into my mouth.

However, in the quest to also shed some lighter upshots to foggy memory, the words, 'Oh sorry, it's menopause brain fog' can sometimes be quite useful, you can always milk it...

- 'Ah sorry I totally forgot I was supposed to be at [insert that thing you didn't want to go to]… bloomin' brain fog'.

- 'Eeeeekk did it start at 7 pm?' She mutters as she turns up at 8:20 pm knowing she'll be home in bed by ten.

- 'I don't remember promising that blow job.' Sorry not sorry.

- 'Oh blimey, did I say I'd run the PTA meeting…my memory!'

- 'I'm so sorry I have a clash I'd forgotten about,' works on anything you may wish to back track on.

- 'Did I forget to go to the gym? Oh.'

Lists help and I like to use those little annoying but useful robots in our home to set reminders. Bullet journaling is my 'go to' method, scribbling on the go, especially in those times when distraction is around and I know the important stuff I'm being told might not sink in. Experiment with supplements or explore brain training games/activities, whatever feels right for you.

If I'm honest I'm just not sure if there's an easy solution, so talking and explaining how it's affecting you with those at home/work/uni is so important.

Coming up with solutions together will make it all bit less meh! I know it feels like Pac-Man is working his way around the brain and slowly zapping all the stuff we need to remember. But it's not 'Game Over,' we've just got to level up and work out how to get through the next mission. Here's some space to write the important stuff...because quite frankly Post-it notes just don't hold their sticky like they used to!

Remember me notes:

Rule 8 Soothe Your Messy Mind

My Menopause, My Journal, My Rules!

Chat through with those around you. What would make it easier for you all to keep things running smoothly (examples could be: everyone adding to the shopping list when something runs out, or using Alexa/Google to set reminders). Write any plans of action here:

ANXIETY IS A BITCH!

Anxiety lives where your thoughts are, either in the future or in the past. Anxiety cannot breathe...when you breathe into the present.

The sick knots in your stomach, that feeling like someone's sitting on your chest, that moment where my stupid brain pivots rapidly as the dense brain fog is sliced through, to make way for the 1,001 overthinking anxious thoughts that build. 'But what if...? Do they think that...? What if I can't...? What if the world ends? Oh God, oh God, oh God.'

In 0.46 seconds I'm catastrophising the worst case scenario possible...I mean FFS, come on, give me a break menopause! Anxious thoughts come and go throughout life. That tummy ache a child complains about? Probably anxiety. The fact that you might go for an airport poo six times? Flight anxiety. But it can go from the usual heightened nervousness to things causing us real problems as we go about our day to day.

When you're in a state of anxiety or overthinking, your brain can go into assumption, jumping to the worst possible scenario. Even from young, when we think someone is talking about, thinking or feeling something about us, we sit in worry. I have to remind myself to stop the chatter and ask, 'what are the actual facts? What do I know to be true?' Because **assumption is different to fact – fact!** When we assume anything, we are making up a story. We don't actually know for sure, so it's not truth. Think about how many times you've done this recently. It's crazy when we realise how many stories we tell ourselves. The truth is that most of the time we're all worrying about what others may be thinking of us, when honestly everyone just worries about themselves! When I find my mind wondering this way I mull over this question or write down **'what do I know to be true?'** Then I can process anything I'm assuming and realise it's simply my mind playing tricks. Let's not ditch intuition here, sometimes we get that strong gut feeling which shouldn't be ignored -–after all, the Chinese call our guts our second brains. When you practise looking at your assumptions it can reduce the anxiety, allowing you to tune in to know when your gut is really sending you a message!

Here's somewhere to scribble when that assumption kicks off to help you focus on what is actually true:

Assumption   *Fact*

LIFE IS LIKE THIS SOMETIMES

Notes:

It's ok to be an over-thinker, it's part of your style. Learning to recognise when you're doing it is the way to make it your own.

Dr John – my therapist

When I heard these words I was like, 'wait what?' Struggling to stop overthinking, this gave me a sense of calm, acknowledging that it's just part of me and that's okay. What I needed was to keep recognising when it's happening and access what I need to do at that point in time, to stop my mind exploring ALL the possibilities. When you have anxiety, your brain overthinks either into a future assumption or tries to relive the past in an unhelpful way. What your brain can't physically or mentally do is overthink what is happening in this precise moment, that's when we're fully in the present. This is the exact moment we have to focus on when we start to feel anxious.

LIGHTER TOUCH BREATHWORK

We covered the conscious connected breathing earlier to aid the physical symptoms and this is the deeper practice that will tap into brain fog, trauma and deeper stress relief. However, because breathwork is an umbrella term for any time we use the breath consciously, even without going deep, it connects us to our mind's health. If you've dabbled with meditation, or other forms of taking a moment to notice your breathing, this is where you have consciously connected your mind to your breath! You might want to explore books, socials and apps or even in-person sessions for this lighter touch approach.

I love the surface level technique, especially if it's with some good beats of music as a guide. I like to do this most mornings and I choose to simply use a free live on Instagram. I like the community feel and it sets up my day beautifully. Connecting to my breath consciously helps me take a moment of gratitude and stop, reduces unhelpful swirling thoughts or when I need something in the moment, like when anxiety hits in the middle of the supermarket!

...AND BREATHE, BRING YOURSELF INTO THE NOW

Here's a few simple in the moment techniques I find work for me. They're not knew, but I like them because, quite frankly, they're the easiest to remember, take no faff and can be done anywhere in any situation. Give them a try should anxiety bubble.

5, 4, 3, 2, 1

→ Start with a slow deep breath in for 5 seconds, hold for 5 and slowly breathe out for 5.

→ Notice 5 things you can see without much effort. The person in front, gum on the pavement, the clouds…

→ Then acknowledge 4 things you can feel. Maybe the bag on your shoulder, your skin on your jumper or the breeze on your face…

→ Try to hear 3 sounds? Distant street noise or someone typing…try to tune in to something that you might not normally acknowledge. The hissing trees, or the heating buzzing. This is where our minds really starts to slow.

→ What are 2 things you can smell? Focus in on a scent, the smell of the train, your pillow if at night, or simply your own skin. Whatever they are breath them in (unless on the tube with an armpit in your face!).

→ Finally, acknowledge either 1 thing you can taste - your last meal, mouthwash, your lipgloss - or 1 positive thing about yourself!

→ Repeat this starting at 5 again as many times as it takes to centre yourself.

BOX BREATHING

This has to be the technique I have used the most and shared with anyone and everyone, even my kids, as it's effective quickly if you're in a bit of a state and doesn't need much thought

```
Look for a square… anywhere! I challenge you now
to do this wherever you are, look up and find
something vaguely square or rectangular. A tile,
a picture, your phone… see! Now focus on that, or
use the arrows on this page.

Move your eyes up one side - breathe in slowly
for 4 through your nose,

Hold for 4, as you move your eyes along the top
of that square

Exhale for 4 (mouth or nose is fine) as your eyes
take you down the other side

Hold without inhaling for 4, as you move across
the bottom of your square, to start again

Repeat a few times until you find yourself
feeling more grounded
```

With both of these techniques, like any others you find, it's no good just trying to pull them out the bag when the anxiety shit hits the fan of panic. You need to practise when you're actually feeling pretty chipper! This allows the memory to cement inside your brain adding it to the emergency response, ready for when it's needed like a safety net.

DON'T TELL ME NOT TO PANIC!

The shear dread, heart palpitations, the 'I actually think I'm going to die' hyperventilating, breathy words coming out of your mouth as the walls close in around you...now that's a panic attack! It can be tremendously scary and can sometimes come out of nowhere, leaving you feeling completely out of control, or that something medical is happening, like a heart attack. Unlike anxiety that tends to linger, bubbling over hours, days or weeks and comes on slowly, building to more intense feelings, panic attacks are like Boom! 'Here I am...now you're listening!' Lasting on average between five to twenty minutes – and in some cases up to an hour – some people may only experience a few in a lifetime, whereas for some it could be a couple of times a week. If these things cross your path, firstly let me say I acknowledge and understand, in the thick of it, how utterly awful it feels and it's hard to find any clarity in what's happening to your mind and body. Secondly, you might feel like you're dying...you are not, and you will be okay. A lot of people go to hospital, especially the first time, so don't beat yourself up if you find yourself in A&E, they have seen many panic attacks in their time.

PREVENTION IS BETTER THAN CURE – GET MINDFUL

Like stress, anxiety and panic are manifestations of our flight or fight response. Mindfulness and meditation are really good preventatives to this all feeling off the scale.

Like the easy techniques I shared, practising even a few minutes a day brings the calming calvary in when those feelings start.

Putting them into action will help take you out of the panic line of fire. This reduces stress and stress is the number one trigger for panic attacks.

Amy Polly, founder of the Mindfulness Rebellion, my mate, and all round rebel in pink, told me, 'Using your breath with intention can activate the para-sympathetic nervous system which is the opposite to fight or flight, releasing calming chemicals into your body. It takes you away from that chemical response, that feeling of danger. So practising mindfulness helps us recognise that what is happening are just thoughts. Even if you get to the stressed state, the thoughts are racing, you can use the breath along with something to focus your mind, like a mantra!'

> In this moment, I am safe and all is well,
> In this moment, I am safe and all is well,
> In this moment, I am safe and all is well.
>
> Amy Polly – Mindfulness Rebellion

Amy also taught me that mindfulness is different to meditation, where you take time to set intent putting yourself in a space of relaxation maybe to music, guided words, chanting or silence. Mindfulness is about noticing, for example, my daily practice is making my morning coffee, I notice the sounds, the feel of the mug, the aromas, the way the coffee hits the cup to the warmth on my skin to the taste in my mouth. Amy says, 'it's simply noticing that brings you into the moment and that's mindfulness. So, practicing this could be put into any activity that you do daily, from brushing your teeth to exercising'.

MEDITATE WITH ME

There are many ways to meditate and whilst a silent retreat in a faraway land sounds utter bliss, when everything is getting on your nerves, it's good to find ways around the time you have and what you're accessible to. There's no doubt that meditation helps in so many ways, it's why it's been practiced for thousands of years. Here's the lightbulb moment: you don't have to buy the incense, sit crossed legged and chant a mantra. You can simply do it whilst boiling the kettle! Take time where you can set an intention for what you need, this could be peace, relaxation or even that niggling feeling you want to acknowledge and allow to pass. Whatever it is, you can meditate from a couple of minutes to hours on end, it's really about where your comfort zone lies. There are some **myths around meditation,** so let's break them down:

- You have to clear your mind. Wrong! Your mind will travel, get distracted, ideas and thoughts will come and go. This is completely normal

- You can only do it at certain times. Incorrect! See what different times suit you. I enjoy a morning meditation, but also have made it part of my bedtime routine. However, if I'm feeling like I need some clarity or I'm enjoying a moment, I'll go off the cuff.

- You have to be religious. Nope! We do see meditation as a practice in some religions, but this is not exclusive, you don't have to believe in anything other than yourself.

- It will always feel peaceful. Simply not. Sometimes you'll feel energised, uncomfortable or a bit aggravated. It depends what's coming up for you, but these are all feelings to acknowledge.

From guided apps or playlists and podcasts to body scans or being part of your yoga practise, there are so many wonderful ways to introduce this into your life. In fact, I challenge you to come knocking and tell me it doesn't help...if you've tried various ways and really given it a shot that is! Persevere, try different things and always make a note about how you felt, or what you are learning about yourself afterwards. I'll give you some reflection space to use as you wish.

Reflection space:

My Menopause, My Journal, My Rules!

Reflection Space

Rule 8 Soothe Your Messy Mind

WHAT'S WITHIN MY GIFT?

Whilst waiting for my HRT implant, there have been times I really wanted to lose it with everyone. So many people said, 'I'd be chasing daily...complaining like mad!' And I did my fair share of chasing and complaining but as the months went on it was affecting my mental health, I was exhausted in the continuous battle against the system, the postcode lottery and a national HRT shortage. Instead, I accepted the process and made peace, however difficult it was to experience the many symptoms. I was alive and there was only so much I *could* control. I had no say over the shortage, huge incompetence, the stretch of the NHS. Although it felt like I was down what felt like a never ending road of ridiculous hurdles, I chose to focus my mind on what *was* within my gift.

Rest, taking time off, using tools I'd learnt to manage my mental health dips, what I fed my body mind and soul and how I would use the energy I did have, is where I focused. Yes, I cried when the consultant failed to show (I waited six hours). Yes, I was gutted and felt guilty to have spent £195 on a private appointment that went nowhere. And yes, I was angry at the whole process (as you may have read earlier) and anxious for my long term health without the hormones. But I had to let that all go and think what is the bigger picture? One of the things that was in my control was how was I going to spend this time waiting?

Luckily for you it was words and thoughts that helped me focus and feel okay at a time that was so challenging...this book might just not have got finished otherwise!

Looking at what's within your circle of influence or control is not anything new, it's an old one but a good one and I just love it as a reminder.

ASKING FOR HELP IS OKAY

Looking for additional help to bring the more mental side of things back in the game is something to consider as you write your own rules to what's going to help. There may be a wait for some mental health support, but don't let that put you off asking. Whilst you're waiting, use helplines, live chats or charities to offload and find a listening ear.

Talking to friends or family, making them aware exactly how you're feeling or thoughts you're having is scary I know, but it'll relieve some pressure allowing them to look out for you when you need it most. You're not a burden, or an inconvenience, and you're not alone.

> Be who you are
> And say how you feel,
> Because those who mind,
> **Don't matter**
> And those who matter,
> **Don't mind.**
> DR SEUSS

There are so many therapies you could try, it's really a case of exploring and having a go. Some more things I've experimented with are:

→ Cognitive Behavioural Therapy (CBT) helps re-wire the brain from unhelpful thoughts, it's believed to be very effective for menopausal mental symptoms, I got a lot out of my sessions, except I was never going to complete the hourly planner they gave me!

→ Hypnotherapy - changes the way we tell ourselves stories and can focus on something specific. Trying this a few times, it's been successful for in the moment things I wanted to work on.

- → Emotional Freedom Technique (EFT), or Tapping, is said to relieve stress and calm and regulate the nervous system by releasing negative thoughts. I didn't get on with this however I know quite a few people who swear by it.

- → Medications. Seek your GP's help to determine whether you'd benefit from these to restore chemical imbalance - some antidepressants even help hot flushes! As mentioned, I didn't go down this route, but I'd never say never.

- → Check out the helplines in the back of the book.

SOMETIMES WE'VE GOT TO SIT IN THE MESS

You might have to ride it. I say this because for some of you, you simply won't be up for trying the meditation, the mindfulness or the practise. Maybe you'll start but things get in the way (like they do) or like me you might get distracted and a bit inconsistent, but you know there are choices to revisit.

If you find something unexpected has come along that conjures up a storm, taking the wind out of your sails and suddenly it's messy, sit there and be vulnerable in this gust of chaos. It's meant to disrupt you. Don't squish it down or try to tidy it away too quickly. Soak it in, it will be painful and so fucking hard at times...or maybe it's beautiful in a weird kind of way. But know you're only there a short while. Things will settle and your next foot forward will be placed. A better thought or feeling will come, and you can pull on the right tools you need when you feel more clear. Be bold while you sit in the mess, let this wind take you. It's all temporary and you are strong enough.

All things must pass.
George Harrison

It's hard to wrap up this section because there's so much more to say or suggest when it comes to our minds. I hope this has allowed you to take a moment to stop, acknowledge and act on how you are feeling right now. Whether on top of the world or feeling like you want it to swallow you up. This is a crazy time that will pass through just as it should, and you will emerge so much more in tune with what your mind needs.

INTERVAL OF EVENTS

The implant saga continues...£195 lighter, the private route wasn't much better. It wasn't two weeks; it didn't happen at all! Taking my money upfront and then unable to get hold of the implant, it was a game of email tennis and I decided to step back. These hurdles were stupid, but I wasn't going to let it consume the little energy I had. So, for now I would wait and hope the NHS list wouldn't be too long.

Handle with Care x

Your Soul

RULE 9

FIND WHAT YOUR *soul needs*

If the moon can move the OCEANS, Imagine what it's doing to US... We're like 65 PER CENT water by the way!

ENCOURAGE THE ENERGY FLOW

Okay, I'm going to get a bit deep, a bit aligned. WTF you might ask? Bear with. Just to confirm, your menopause (however it landed at your door) is not all doom and gloom. It's actually pretty fucking awesome. Here's why. **When one thing changes, stops or disappears, it makes space for something new – growth.** It's that little something we've not realised we needed, that idea or spark and, as my friend says, it allows time for that something to percolate! I guess you could say I've always felt connected to something, whether the universe, the deep conversation with a stranger in a queue, or that feeling you get when everyone is singing the same song at an epic gig. I like to think our bodies are entwined with both the earth and what we see when we look up. How else could it be? Whatever your spiritual, cultural or religious views, we are and always will be connected as humans. We're a force of energy in and out of flow with the earth on our skin, water penetrating our pores, wind causing havoc with that hairstyle (we actually had time for), even with what we see in the sky – and, of course, each other.

Although we're the same energy, we're aligned to some things more than we are to others. This is why we attract our people...our tribe! It's why some of us like the grass under our toes, yet others relish in running their fingers on the cool hard concrete in a city building. This isn't to start a debate on beliefs and get into a chapter on all things universe, God or in-between. I most certainly don't have the answers and this, after all, is a book about menopause. But how is it that we are all so beautifully different...and yet somehow here you are, reading this with me as I write. We are aligned already in a frequency of energy; **I already know you're my kind of person and I yours...we're literally on the same page!**

ENERGY'S CONNECTION TO CHANGE

At times since my surgery, when things have got nasty and my health has been disrupted, that feeling of flow has become sticky and blocked. It wasn't until I was at my bare bones that I realised healing the mental and physical sides of me was only going to get me so far. I had to reach into my soul, looking within to heal and amplify areas of my being that maybe felt like a nice to do before, this became a downright necessity. I started to look up and outward, widening the lens on how I saw this stage of my life. I became curious about things that felt far away from textbooks and prescriptions. Things like the moon intrigued me. I thought surely if it could move our oceans it could shift something within me. After all we're sixty-five per cent water, right? I'd heard of moon cycles and wondered what happens when you didn't have a womb anymore or periods, or when someone is peri-menopausal? And what about my Sacral Chakra…where did that go when I bid farewell of my internal organs? I'd always been in tune with my body, with the pain and learning how to manage. I wondered how I'd done that? Where had that come from? And yet somehow my views and voice had reflected other's beliefs not my own. I'd been connected to my physicality, but I wasn't aligned to who I was, my true purpose and wisdom, I guess. Maybe it was because I wasn't ready, maybe menopause makes you ready? With medicine and HRT feeling not so reliable, I thought to myself 'there must be something to help plug the gap.'

I've had many conversations with hundreds of women of varying professions, ages and cultures, all in different stages of their own menopause, and it struck me that for most, they all have this inner spirit, this inner oomph. They have this deeper knowing that they're part of a shift that's bigger than them and however difficult menopause is for some of these women, something stirs.

Erupting inner questions, or exploration, it's a time where women start looking inside themselves for answers. Maybe because at times we're left not knowing what's happening or maybe it really is **as big as womanhood?**

It might be taking moments to breathe through something, or the calming smoke of incense, the odd crystal finds itself in your home, or you find solace in really feeling into the nature on your walks. It could be that your inner self starts to shout, 'I'm not going to be silenced' and the freedom to say what you want or need begins to surface and flourish…

you start to stride forward. Your body, mind and soul are somehow working together, and these things creep into your life rituals. All these are times you're connecting to your self and your own energy, consciously or unconsciously, encouraging the flow.

It's no coincidence that suddenly we might want a change, an epiphany comes about that relationship or the job that doesn't make us happy. It might feel like we've had enough, and the fire in your belly rises. This menopause is changing so much it's inevitable that there is a shift in consciousness within, that has created the capacity to awaken a new, bolder you!

My own mum pretty much got on with her peri-menopause until crippling panic attacks took over and she went for therapy. After some inner work she had a sought of re-awakening. Through exercise and night classes her confidence grew, she'd just go do her thing whether my dad was up for it or not! She didn't need permission or company, she found her voice, ramped up the adventure and even travelled Australia alone for three weeks, leaving fifteen year old me with my Dad and a freezer full of well-prepared nourishing dinners, so to avoid the mountain of take-away cartons upon her return (I'm not bitter)! She stepped into something marvellous and now definitely lives doing what she wants without waiting for the approval of anyone. I didn't see it at the time, of course, but I see it now. I couldn't help but wonder if women (before modern medicine) had always had this 'stepping up into themselves' experience when entering this change in their lives. Were there bigger powers at play here, that we've either had censored or we have not been open to in the constant state of busy or the ramble of society?

HISTORY LESSON...

There's some interesting stuff on the history of menopause, here's my take on it all for a bit of fun!

Let's get our black bin liners and pointy hats on and start with witches! Before you think have the lack of hormones finally got to her? There's a link...well, I think so anyway! In old English, the word Witch means 'Wicca' or 'Wise One'. These women were mostly older and were accused of evil sorcery, pagan worship and black magic and their herbal healing knowledge was feared as Christianity spread. They would serve their communities with homeopathic treatments helping women through their cycles and childbirth. However, it was thought that once their bleeding stopped, they became prone to accusations of Witchcraft and they'd be blamed for stillbirths, illness or miscarriages...all seen as a curse.

Living over fifty in the mid 1400's was rare. It's interesting to picture the dark hairs growing out of chins, wrinkling dull skin and sunken eyes through lack of sleep, along with thinning hair, achy joints affecting posture and a curiousness to heal one's self and others. Throw that together with their connection with the moon, that big old thing called energy, and having a chat with your mates over a sage tea...it's easy to see how that meant you MUST have been a witch! Even broomsticks are real peeps...okay, they didn't fly on them, but they would be used to cleanse a room ready for healing!

These poor souls were burnt at stakes or hanged, their furry four-legged companions watching at the side lines, faintly meowing goodbye, perhaps simply because of the change. Witch hunts in modern day could be seen as the patriarchy shitting it over menopausal women! They were non-conformers, healers, connected to self and to their divine feminine – their inner pussy power... they sound right up my street to be honest! They were a threat. Remember learning about 'Salem' at school? Well, thirteen, of the sixteen witches were no longer fertile!

Thank goodness we've moved on from these scary scenes and yes, the patriarchy still needs some work, but at least we have waxing, tweezers and a good chiropractor we can call.

So, next time a crooked figure enters your screen on a Disney movie, or even a bad tempered step-mother jealous of the younger, fertile and carefree singing character, spare a thought, show some empathy, she's probably still waiting for her HRT!

It was in **1821** that the word 'la menopause' (menopause) was first used by Dr Charles Pierre Louis de Gardanne. It's thought that this derived from various ancient Greek words: 'men' meaning month and closely related to the word moon (the months were measured by the moon), and 'pauein' which means to stop. So, the monthlies stop. We then moved on to French doctors who liked to call menopausal women 'des Reines detronees' meaning 'the unthroned queens'...twats!

In the 1930s people started describing it as a deficiency disease – they were on the nugget with deficiency at least. Various replenishment therapies continued to be experimented with including testicular juice and the crushed ovaries of animals – excuse me while I spew in my mouth!

It's the change of life...the critical time.

Edward John Tilt – English Physician 1815-1893

Moving on to the **Victorians,** Tilt wrote one of the first known books on menopause, stating there were around 100 symptoms, all of which could be treated by a doctor. Remedies included things like a nice bath, a glass of sherry, Opium or the odd chloroforming...jeez! The Victorians, obsessed with medicine, turned menopause into an illness, linking it to a mental imbalance then conjuring all manner of terrible acts to suppress 'the madness'. They coupled the physical womb with the brain, rather than separating hormonal changes and mental illness that in fact had nothing to do with whether you had a vagina or not!

Suddenly women became **hysterical!** Hysteria comes from the Greek word, hystera, which translates to the English word uterus. The condition of hysteria historically described extreme changes in mood, emotions and behavioural response in women, this again cementing the perceived link between the womb and the brain.

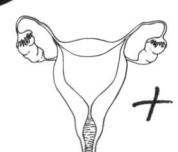

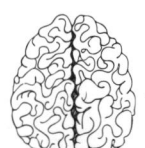

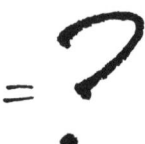

It was not until **1966** that gyneacologist Robert A. Wilson claimed that Estrogen replacement therapy should be taken... hurrah! He wrote, '...with HRT a woman's breast and genital organs will not shrivel, she will be much more pleasant to live with and will not become dull and unattractive'. Oh Rob, you were doing so well.

Bring on the late **1990s** in the USA and the first clinical trials on HRT showed that in the small number of testers, and after only the first set of results were published, that HRT was showing detrimental effects. This spread fear amongst the medical profession and although the research is not conclusive, it caused a huge decline in HRT usage and that ripple effect still lingers today.

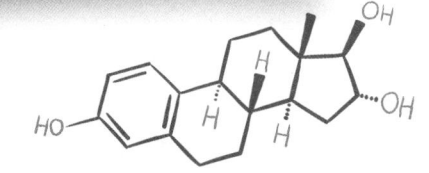

The dawn of the internet and socials

has now given menopause a voice and those experiencing it a platform to learn, share and connect. Along with education and up to the minute research, the online world carries misinformation and differing views, so it can feel pretty overwhelming. However, it does provide choice, and we can be empowered to decide for ourselves what resonates with us personally and advocate for ourselves instead of trusting that guy with the Opium!

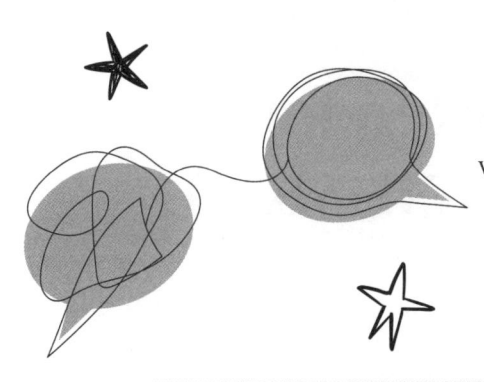

You can see how over the years there's a huge wedge of disconnection between the growth of knowledge and expertise within medical intervention and science, and what's happening energetically, that wholesome alignment to self. The latter has perhaps been lost in history.

WHAT'S NEXT???

Rule 9   Find What Your Soul Needs

CLAIM BACK THE CONNECTION TO SELF

It's time to take that lost connection back, and as the Greeks seem to keep it simple, let's use their definition of energy.

ENERGY IN GREEK = ENERGIA

FROM

EN ➡ IN, WITHIN

ERGON ➡ WORK

It's more than meditation, it's inner work peeps!

Doing all the things we've talked about so far to build your toolkit for your own set of rules is great, but establishing the energy around these things and how you open your soul to receive them is a different thing altogether. It was my first ever sound bath that I got my, 'wow, this is what it's all about moment'. I could see the colours behind my closed eyes, I could feel how my body was reacting to the vibrations and, somehow, I was seeing visions, messages, words...I questioned, 'what was that?'

The answers are often found beneath our own skin.

Intrigued, I experimented with this more, trying different things; sound healing, Reiki, women's circles, crystal work and I even visited a retreat. I preferred some of these more than others and the feelings would vary each time, from calm to agitation to sometimes feeling weird or even profound. I wouldn't always get a clear answer to whatever it was I was seeking, but somehow, I knew that in time that would come. As I tried all these differing approaches one thing ran through them all; I realised that treating menopause with modern HRT, building strength at the gym and therapy for the mind is all amazing, but what did my soul need? Was this what I was grappling for to complete the jigsaw? I now realise that once you can start to listen to your inner self, you level up in moving through menopause, finding more peace with who you are. And I promise you don't need to jet off to Bali, spend a penny or overcomplicate it at all.

Have you ever been with a **crowd** at a concert or sporting match… all collectively singing, chanting… feeling **connected?** That is that is **energy, spiritual,** it's like a **collective prayer** between strangers and it's **magic!**

TRY THIS...

- Put any music on that you feel drawn to and sit, or lay down where comfortable.

- Close your eyes, take three long breaths in through your nose and out through your mouth.

- Focus on the space between your eyes, you may start to see colours.

- Set an intention - this is something you want to bring into your life or let go of, or both. You might be asking a question or visualising yourself in a certain situation. Then let it float away. Try not to overthink this.

- Then just listen and feel the music within your body mind and soul until the end of the song.

What sensations did you feel?

Rule 9   Find What Your Soul Needs

My Menopause, My Journal, My Rules!

What things did you see?

These notes may not make sense, or they could really resonate. Just jot them down and be grateful for this time. Do this whenever you need to bring things back to yourself or what you need. By exploring this more and more, you'll find a depth during self care or new activities. You'll feel more connected to your soul, listening to your heart when the brain is getting all sensible. As time goes on your energy will align, not only from within but you'll notice those around you too. This might even start to draw in what you unconsciously need more of and move you away from things or people that don't serve you anymore.

Write any words or messages that came up:

This can feel uncomfortable, bizarre and challenging, I get it. We're not used to this way, we've all those years of history steering us away from what's within us. We're also impatient, wanting immediate answers, but this is about trusting in yourself and understanding that what's meant for us doesn't always present how we want it to. The great thing is, you can do this anywhere and it doesn't just have to be when things are difficult or we're in a frenzy craving clarity. Sometimes I find myself just closing my eyes to feel the energy around me, to soak in all the good vibes.

If you've got some time and budget to spare, have a look at working with a sound healer, reiki master or any other therapist in this space that you feel drawn to. Go with what feels like your vibe, your intuition is powerful.

GET YOUR 'NO FUCKS GIVEN' HAT ON!

Slight warning: I may have broken the F bomb record in this section… Just saying!

Once you learn to step further into your own power it becomes easier to tackle things that come along, in a way that will really serve you. A week that's challenged you, or you feel a bit beaten, whatever your mantra or means is to help get you to a good place, remember that at some point you've got to put yourself first, get diggity with what your soul needs and decide which fucks you're going to give out!

From the moment we open our eyes in the morning, we're faced with things that require us to give a fuck! Mine usually starts with my left boob hitting the floor before my feet as I creak out of bed, only to turn right into a full-length mirror and think, 'Hey, hot stuff'. We're told, expected and pressured to give a fuck about a lot and usually it starts with the internal stuff or how we perceive our bodies, intelligence, confidence, etc. The trouble is, we give ourselves copious amounts, almost an endless pit, of fucks to just give away to those who jibe, judge or criticise. We take some from ourselves too with negative self talk, zero compassion and, quite frankly, not being that nice to ourselves. So, what if you told yourself there were only so many fucks in your bucket? What would you do? I reckon you'd be a bit more careful about what and who you gave them too.

Love note: this isn't about being rude, mean or selfish, it's choosing where you spend your hoots! Whether during swimwear shopping hell (me), the new muffin top protruding, vs sipping on a cold drink over the scenery of your dreams on holiday. Or letting the wind blow through your hair at the roller disco vs staying at home, because you think you might look like a twat! Even asking to sit by the open window in your meeting to stay cool delivering your ideas vs staying quiet so as not to upset/annoy/look weird whilst sweating your genius thoughts into your Powerpoint... you hear me right?

It's time to re-define where your thought energy gets spent, what's worth a mindset shift and what you can send up in smoke. The things that steal away your fucks may be deep rooted and reoccurring or surface level –like a fleeting comment from a stranger. Once you think about only having limited fucks to give, your brain will re-wire when choosing what is deserving of them. So how do you do it? Great question.

HERE LIES all the FUCKS I GAVE

Rule 9 Find What Your Soul Needs

TIME TO BURN... NO REALLY!

Changing our thoughts takes time and practise, reminders to tell ourselves new stories, learning to be a bit more conscious of what's zapping us and our self esteem. However, there is also power in a little ritual. Something that signifies a change, a moment where an action you've taken can ingrain in your memory (brain fog depending). This acts like an event anchor, when you're about to spill out all your fucks to 'that Karen' on Facebook!

Doing something poignant also helps us heal a little more, by acknowledging the things we've given so much energy to when it's been detrimental to ourselves.

What I'm about to ask you to do is well worth the investment of: writing, buying the matches and the effort to find somewhere safe to burn the unnecessary fucks you're giving! Yep, you read right, we're literally going to burn this shit!

As I stood outside, with my bare feet to the ground, Diana guided us, each holding our pieces of paper. We'd only been at her retreat for a day, and we'd already tapped deep, reaching in to understand what was holding us back; what things we needed to let go of. The painful things, grief, even surface trauma, and realising just how much could be written about where or who we were giving our now limited fucks to.

I was so emotional standing in this circle of women, literally watching these parts of ourselves go up in flames. Diana, this spiritual, singing, heart-centred soul, the type of person you could melt into as she encapsulates your energy with her sound to heal, had introduced us to, in her words, 'The Fuck It Bucket'! Amongst the smoke of each other's demons, I read my words aloud, hands slightly shaking and emotion trembling off my tongue before adding mine to the flames. It was a simple moment that I will never forget, a turning point, and one that I anchor back to when I'm giving too many hoots to something that just doesn't deserve any. I do this every so often, it's not a one-time thing, it's inevitable that life happens and we need to reset the boundaries with ourselves, so I wanted to encourage you to do the same.

THE RITUAL

1. Using the 'Fuck It Bucket' pages at the back, write down all the things you're giving your energy to, or giving a hoot about, that you know you need to let go of. These are things that have taken your emotions or time and despite them making you feel pants, you've still invested. Go deep within, it might be guilt, opinions, or things you hold with regret. It can be words, sentences, doodles, names, whatever, you'll know in the moment. Trust yourself and listen to what comes up. Connecting with this stuff and being able to release it in a physical way is some powerful shizzle to sizzle.

2. Purge complete, rip out the page and take it outside. No need for a full moon, half moon, or any moon; to be fair as long as it's not pissing down with rain, you're alright.

3. Read aloud what's on your paper...feel it deeply; then, when you're ready, light that baby up by tossing it into a ready-made fire, chiminea, bbq, whatever you've got, and watch it burn.

4. Feel whatever you need to, watch the smoke rise and try to imagine those thoughts physically leaving you. Feel the energy in that moment.

SAFETY NOTE: because we're all adults here, please only play safely with matches! Do this outside and away from: little people, animals or numpties that would fall into the flames of your deepest thoughts. A trip to A&E is not part of this healing ritual. Health and safety check over.

You, my dear, are letting that shit go...

...I'm so proud of you.

You'll begin to notice more when you're reaching for one of your precious fucks and the more you become aware, the more you'll think about whether it's warranted. Negative self-doubt becomes 'let's do the thing' or when a dig about looking a little chubbier from that joker at work comes, you might reply, 'thanks Marcus, yeah gives me more to play with when I wank!'. Ok maybe not if Marcus is your boss...but your head can revel in the thought!

> Love note: this isn't a substitute for doing the hard and deep work through therapy for trauma, mental illness or very low mental health. Believe me, you'll benefit from being with professionals. This is simply learning to release some things that are weighing you down right now. It's allowing you to make way for things that you should care about and it feels a bit magical too.

So, what happens now you've released some negatives and made way for the good stuff? It's time to think about what this stage of your life is going to bring you. What do you want? Who are you now? What lights you the hell up? Menopause, we've established, is not the end, so now is the time to up-level.

Note to my Mum: I've washed my mouth out with soap and donated the contents of my swear jar to a menopause awareness charity... forgive me

V x

What lights me up? Gets me excited? What do I love, makes me laugh, or my heart full? Write it down here:

Rule 9   Find What Your Soul Needs

MANIFESTING

I know you're thinking, this isn't about 'the change', but you see it kind of is. We've made physical, mental and somewhat soulful shifts and it was about this time that I started to question, well what now? What's next on the path? **How do I start to bring what I want to the table to fill this next stage in my life?**

You may be climbing to the top of your career game or maybe you've realised the explorer within is still there. But how do you make it happen? I'm a big believer that we do have to do some graft, putting ourselves in situations of opportunity, and say yes to things that scare us. Burnout also taught me that hard work is something that has been fed down to us, 'work hard, play hard' and all that. But ask yourself this: why should doing or being what you desire be so difficult? If it's something that's meant for us, it will already be within our gift, our talent, or on its way, if we truly believe and trust.

To manifest is to bring something into your life that you desire. It's focusing on what you would like, not what you wouldn't. It's tuning into your heart and asking, **'What do I really desire? What would that really feel like?'** Once you have that set, it's letting it go for the universe to do its thing. Check out this ancient manifesting craft, I'm merely giving you a snippet, but, put simply, it's trusting the universe to deliver what your heart desires. This is usually superior to what your head thinks you want or thinks you need, and you have to be honest with yourself on what comes with your manifesting package. There's no point in dreaming to be a famous actress if, in your heart, you want your life to remain just as it is, where you can shop for your Tena lady and no-one cares! Seems brutal, but you need this honesty when tuning into your real desires, so your dreams can be as big as you really want them to be.

Making space is imperative, cluttering your life with stuff you don't want leaves little room for the things you want to bring in. Let's say you've always dreamed of a road trip, but just never seem to have enough money and time; you're waiting for the prices to drop.

Ask yourself, have you even allowed for the time off? Are you saying yes to things that take your time and money that you don't even care for? Where are the brochures on your coffee table and researched route notes? Did you just go to the same holiday destination three times and spend the money the road-trip would have cost? So, how much do you really want it? Maybe the universe isn't delivering that cheaper flight because it's a bit confused as to whether you actually desire it at all!

Take some time to think about what you truly desire, ask yourself why? Make a few notes if it helps.

CREATE YOUR VISION

In 2021 I created my first ever vision board and this book was on it. Alongside a picture of Chris Hemsworth with his shirt off, I'd look at pictures of: doodled covers, someone holding a journal in a quaint little book shop and an author at a festival. Closing my eyes, I could almost feel it in my hands, the weight, texture, really tuning in to how I would want you to feel holding it too. I knew one day I'd create it, so others felt less alone. Visualising myself as an author, way before that job title was official, I kept the vision close all the time, but let go of the wanting and just trusted. When my body was going through hell, I finally learnt to let go of the negative feelings about my health and there I was filling up the crack, learning about becoming an indie author, helping people and researching. I realised that my life wasn't a 'what could have been story', it was 'my story', and that my vision was to share it to help others. And here we are, my book in your hands, how cool is that? And although I'm yet to snog the Hemsworth, it's amazing what we're capable of when we step into what lights us up. This thing called menopause is happening. Whatever it's serving you in terms of symptoms or has taken away from the path that you thought was yours... **you have the power to make a new vision, a new story and you owe it to yourself to make it happen!**

TIME TO GET FUNKY AND CREATE SOMETHING VISUAL.

Whatever your artistic capabilities, having the things you desire where you can see them keeps the mind focused and also sorts out the keepers from the stuff you realise is not for you. Doodle, use words, print beautiful pictures or, if you prefer digital, maybe use Pinterest to represent your vision, goals and the things you want to bring in. Fill the next double page or go big on the fridge, your call.

So many women I've talked to see menopause as an ending. But I've discovered this is your moment to **REINVENT YOURSELF** after years of focusing on the needs of everyone else. It's your opportunity to **GET CLEAR ABOUT WHAT MATTERS TO YOU** and then to **PURSUE THAT WITH ALL YOUR ENERGY, TIME AND TALENT.**

Oprah Winfrey

My Vision Board

TAKE ACTION

You've got the manifesting down, the vision board is up, so why is nothing happening? The universe is powerful, but it won't hand you things on a plate. Just listing goals won't cut it either. Instead, focusing on smaller achievable actions is a more effective way to make stuff happen. Accountability is also key; we're just more likely to keep going if we have somene tapping on our shoulder.

Look at your vision pages and choose one thing you desire more than anything. Brain dump all the things you need to do, learn or ask for to edge closer. Find the goals within the vision, for example, you'd love that marathon medal, but you're yet to run at all. So, your goal might be to jog one mile, taking you closer to your vision. What do you need to do to get to that first goal? Turning these goals into smaller actionable steps builds a plan, you'll be moving forward (towards that dream house/holiday/partner), without feeling it's too big or overwhelming. Agree accountability with someone or a group who'll challenge and support your vision. Do this for your whole board or take one at a time, building from one smaller goal to the next.

By creating action you're sending a clear energetic message out. Think of it as eighty per cent personal action, leaving twenty per cent for the universe to work it's magic!

Recap:

- Choose one thing you desire and brain dump everything associated
- Find the smaller goals within this vision
- Plot out the actions into a plan
- Accountability!
- Have the courage to keep going
- Trust the universe to deliver the rest

Holding the courage to keep at it and enjoy the journey, including all the times you feel you may have failed, is important too. When that vision becomes a reality it will feel amazing, however in reality that feeling will be fleeting, and before you know it you'll be onto the next. So, soak in each smaller milestone, you'll thank yourself for it.

Once clear, note your goals down and who you're accountable to use your braindump / actions pages in the back to keep close to them.

ENTERING QUEENHOOD

This is a physical transition, a mental awakening (or slog), a soul journey to reconnection and a time where we can ask ourselves, 'what do we need to sack off and what is bringing us joy?' There is so much going on as you learn to own the entirety of yourself and make your own damn rules about how you're going to ride this time. Yes, it's like you're stepping into another phase of adulthood that no-one mentioned, but there's wisdom and synchronicity with you now, that may not have been there before. It's like prior to menopause we were a 'queen in training'.

I once heard someone say, 'imagine it's like stepping into our Queen selves, through the initiation of menopause'…how cool is that? This embodies all the changes, the mess and the mindset shifts, to step up and let go of everything holding us back. This can be so powerful. Just getting comfortable to sit with ourselves through all our choices, changes and learns, we adapt to release the 'should haves' opening space for what capabilities we hold. **We're stepping into Queenhood!**

I understand this term may not resonate with you, there may be a metaphor that fits better for what you feel, but however you see this; breakthrough, graduation, coming into your power moment, make note and soak it in, because this is the new beginning.

Reflections/Goals/Actions

Reflections/Goals/Actions

'SHE'S CHANGED...IT'S JUST THE MENOPAUSE'

This is simply not true. Maybe you've decided that you're no longer going to tolerate the bullshit! It's a reckoning; you're waking up to yourself, to what really matters as you filter out the unnecessary. Leaving your soul with what it now desires, you're gaining clarity.

It's not 'just the menopause,' it's alignment to a sense of integrity, respect for your body, your whole being and for the sisterhood around you. You can love on yourself harder, be present in the moments that bring happiness, and you'll walk so much more confidently through joy and fulfilment.

So, to go full circle, perhaps we *are* a bit witchy! Maybe we *do* step into a realisation that 'we're coming home to ourselves at this time'. Perhaps wisdom doesn't come with age at *all,* delivering menopause to us all at different times ...simply because we're now ready.

Perhaps it's not that she's changed. **MAYBE** she just stopped **GIVING A SHIT** about what doesn't light her up!

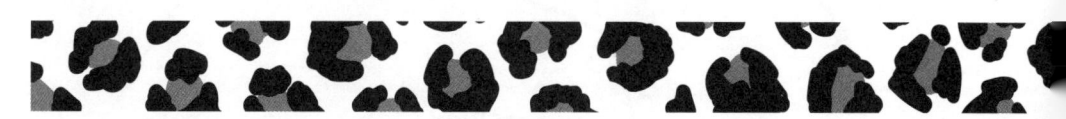

they will listen

RULE 10

Enlighten Your *Loved Ones*

There is something incredibly empowering about having all the knowledge you need, but knowing how to weave that into just a normal chat at dinner, at work or down the aisle in Aldi...that's where change happens!

One of the main things we hear is that **we should 'have the conversation'** and I believe this is starting to happen. What I observe is that we're still very comfortable to stay within our safety net with this conversation, only opening up to those experiencing it directly and finding solace in those heartfelt shares or rants with each other. How do we reach outside this safe place, extending to an audience that at present have no clue? You may be super comfortable chatting about all the intricate details, or you might feel that you'd prefer to be more private – there's no right or wrong, and we should show empathy to both camps. Holding space for everyone to work through their own personal experience, on their own agenda if necessary, is why you're here writing your own rules, doing it your way.

don't sugar coat the truth unless it's on a doughnut!

TALKING ABOUT MENOPAUSE

Most of us don't spend that much time in our homes, as work/education holds most of our weekly hours. We're great at holding stuff in where we need to and it's often those we live with or our closest friends and family that get the brunt with no explanation when symptoms are driving us doo-lally. It's here I'll start, because these relationships are quite honestly the ones that really matter. We have a tendency to build our own barriers in sharing what's going on with us physically or emotionally in menopause. So, I'm going to keep this really simple:

There really is nothing that you can say about the menopause that is going to do long term harm to anyone.

Whether it be educating the young ones around you to tackling the hard to have chats within your relationship, or talking to the people you work with, everyone, in the long run, will be better off for knowing just a bit more.

THOSE WE LOVE

I'm talking partners and close friends here, because both hold equal weighting depending on your personal situation. Firstly, these people love us, they should want the best for us and I'm pretty sure if they're good ones they'll want to know how they can support you. I'm not going to sit here and deny that I've lost my shit with the hubs more than once; the words, 'If you want to be mothered…off you pop back to yours', 'I already have two children, I don't need a third,' and even, 'you may have painted the kitchen twice in nine years, but I've cooked in it every fucking day… so step up to the hob!' have indeed fallen out of my mouth. There are endless anecdotes I could share and I'm sure you'll relate to few, but we have always kept communicating, because, actually he's a total saint at most things and I'm far from perfect myself. Learning, discussing, compromising and a lot of patience is why, I guess, we're still at it nearly twenty-five years in. Reframing some of these convos, making it more about 'us' rather than 'self', is something I'm understanding more and noticing positive differences.

Communication with those you love is going to give you a sense of security, a sounding board to share your worries and will help break open the things you need to get off your chest; which might just have a knock on affect to the other areas in your life. Helping your partner or close friends to understand symptoms, your frustrations, or just why you might lose it occasionally, invites them into what's going on. Not waiting until you blow your top to do it...now that's something else!

What you need to share is yours, it's different for us all so try to think about what you'd like to say to your nearest and dearest and write the words below - don't hold back:

You may have a huge list and this might feel overwhelming, so it's time to break it down.

Look through what you've written. What is there that you really need to address? This is a good place to start. Write that one thing underneath with some ideas of how and when you could talk about this.

It might be you'll chat it through, or maybe write a note to them if easier, find a way to say what you need in a way that works for them too.

Rule 10   Enlighten Your Loved Ones

With the rest, try to split this up in to smaller groups below.

- What am I feeling?

- What am I finding difficult?

- What do I need?

- What will help?

Sometimes the conversation doesn't have to be words. It can be signposting to a podcast or website that tackles the subject, or quizzing the person in question to find out how many symptoms they know. This isn't all on you remember, encourage them to be curious in finding out, or simply show the words I've written in a letter later on, just for them.

Once you've segmented these thoughts you may feel clearer, seeing what warrants a conversation and how you could approach this. Work through the boxes, crossing out anything that already feels dealt with because you've got it off your chest with written words. Then focus on what remains. Often we find what's in these boxes relate to each other, for example, we feel scared of something because we feel a certain way about what we're finding difficult. Linking in what is helping you already gives you flow and purpose when going into the convo. Pick your timing, be empathetic, this might be the first time they're hearing this and give them the light at the end of whatever you're sharing. What I mean by this is, we're all hyper tuned in to 'WIIFM' (What's In It For Me)! It's human nature, so I try to remember this when explaining what's going on for me to someone who might not necessarily see it through the same lens.

We spend so much energy trying to win people round to our way of thinking or feeling and right now you might just not have that to spare. So, sharing the light in this circumstance means illuminating something that will make their ears prick up, playing into their needs as well as yours. Without demanding, 'I need this...' or, 'you don't get it...' or 'you don't understand...', instead use the boxes as a framework to help you articulate what you need to say. 'This is how I feel...it's difficult because... but what really helps me is when you...' Big up the stuff they do that really helps and play to their strengths when asking them to support in ways they might not have done up to now. I know what you're thinking, 'why the hell should I massage their ego?' I get it, I really do, but let's just put our own ego aside for a minute.

This isn't a competition over who is more righteous to moan about the chores, this is about getting what *you* need to help make the areas of your life which menopause impacts easier...simple! It doesn't make you less of a feminist or kick-ass human. It allows you to learn differing ways to approach things, and ultimately everyone comes out the other side more knowledgeable, connected and happy!

Move the rocks, have the conversation

TELL THE LITTLE ONES

Ditch the complication, children are curious (isn't that wonderful?) and honestly, how much cooler is it to capture that curious streak, lap it up and answer their questions honestly, before they enter into an adult world where curiosity gets squished away by busy lives! My biggest tips are simply:

- ✓ Call your body parts their proper names
- ✓ Explain matter-of-factly what is happening biologically
- ✓ For emotional/mental symptoms, explain and name the feelings connected to menopause. Reassure them, 'it's not your fault that I might get angry', for example
- ✓ Talk about what you do or where you go to help your physical and mental health
- ✓ As you're learning symptoms, they can too… they're never too young

This does a few things. 1) Gives them the opportunity to learn about their own body, 2) understand that it's not just a physical change, 3) helps them know that if they feel a certain way mentally, physically or emotionally, they too can ask or find help. These are all great life lessons.

CHAT TO THE TEENS

Now I've always been incredibly open with both the kids about all the conversations as a parent you never really want to have! As I hit surgical menopause, my daughter was entering the biggest hormonal changes of her life so far. Blimey, it was like a hurricane at times when our clashes erupted, leaving mass destruction as the lads of the house crept amongst the shadows to avoid us! As you can imagine, I talk a lot about the M word, so I was looking forward to sitting down with her and getting her thoughts on it all, without prompting, just letting her share all her knowledge. She was fifteen at the time, and this convo didn't come out of the blue, by the way. We sat in a cafe over a hot chocolate and this is how it went…I kid you not.

Me: So, tell me what you know about menopause.

Sloth-teen: It's a woman thing! I don't really care because it doesn't affect me at this time

Me: What age do you think you go into it?

Sloth-teen: Like 40

Me: What actually happens to you?

Sloth-teen: You can't have babies anymore... you get shouty and it annoys me when you forget things (I realise we're talking about me now). It's like, how can you forget what I literally said the other day and you're getting worse (she's definitely venting)!

Me: What age do you think people should learn about it?

Sloth-teen: I don't think there's much point to learn it at school. The majority won't care.

Me: Where would you go if you were experiencing symptoms?

Sloth-teen: I'd go to the doctors.

Me: What if I told you that doctors don't have to learn about menopause (this was true at the time), even though half the population will go through it at some point.

Sloth-teen: I'd search on YouTube!

Conversation ends, with her telling me she's hungry and bored!

Was I shocked? Did I immediately self reflect thinking **what the actual fuck?** Of course I did! She knows how old I am right? What about all the talks, the explanations the bloomin' TikTok videos of mine she's 'liked'. Had it not gone in? Then I realised, this wasn't about me. She was being honest in her thoughts about what reactions her friends might have at school, that maybe it wasn't that important for her to have this conversation right now or maybe she was just in need of toast! My point is, don't **not** talk to the teens for fear of their reaction. My two have definitely winged about me talking vulvas on socials because I'm, 'soooooo embarrassing' and their friends follow me. But I've challenged asking, 'why do they think your friends might follow? Maybe their Mum is in menopause, perhaps they're worried about something themselves'.

However I also know they do share this knowledge passed down. The Boy once told his friend's mum that I was writing a book on menopause because I went through it younger than most. She confided saying she was peri-menopausal and he went on to ask her, 'how are you getting on with it all?'. So we should definitely give our kids the space to share the trinkets of wisdom we give them, when it feels right for them.

We know teenagers are in a world of their own, we might have to catch them on a sociable day, but keep feeding the knowledge bit by bit, whatever their gender. Because I'm sure some of it will be absorbed. And here's why it's so important to question your daughters, your nieces, your sisters, not just for what they'll meet in decades ahead, but also what might be happening around them now…

Hello I'm Natasha..

Magazines, Make-up But No Menstruation

At thirteen we'd be reading 'Just Seventeen' and 'Smash Hits' magazines, chatting over that latest band, doing the, 'what your star sign says about you' quiz and looking at what the next fashion trend was. As my mates hid tampons up their sleeves at school, mine stayed put in the depths of my school bag unused. Instead, I was having hot flushes and horrendous migraines, with no sign of me starting my period. I felt like a complete freak. My family moved about a lot, so as each school move happened, opportunities in asking 'is this normal?' moved too. For over ten years I held that question, my secret.

It was in my twenties that I heard the words, 'premature ovarian failure', trying to take it in, sat there with the man of my dreams as the doctor handed us a leaflet for IVF. Finally having no periods and feeling different made sense. I'd opened up to my boyfriend Damian for the first time a few months before. I was petrified and almost gave him permission to find and love someone 'normal'. Confiding in him how I'd never had a period and how terrified I felt I couldn't have kids, he reassured me saying, 'I love you for you, not what you can give me, whatever happens, we'll get the support we need'. I'd felt so lonely for so long and this was the start of a freedom to own my body, being open and living (however hard) my honest life. We said, 'I do,' and for us, adoption felt right. Two siblings came into our life to love and nurture.

Learning to cope with the infertility, the continuous symptoms - without HRT - and the emotional trauma that had wrapped around those years are all top of the list of support I wished I'd had. If only there was counselling support and knowledge from a younger age. I look at my daughter and I hope things change for her... for future generations.

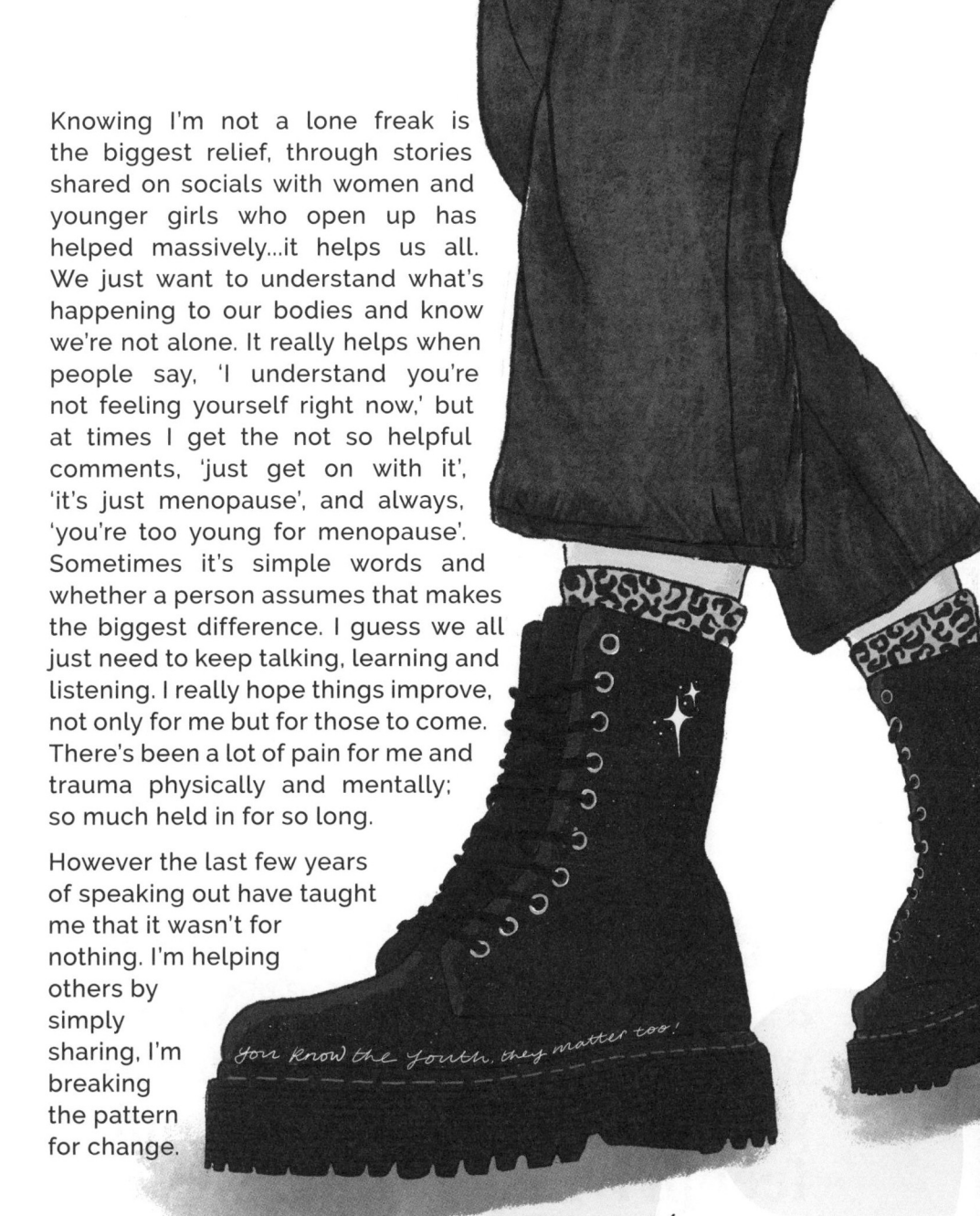

Knowing I'm not a lone freak is the biggest relief, through stories shared on socials with women and younger girls who open up has helped massively...it helps us all. We just want to understand what's happening to our bodies and know we're not alone. It really helps when people say, 'I understand you're not feeling yourself right now,' but at times I get the not so helpful comments, 'just get on with it', 'it's just menopause', and always, 'you're too young for menopause'. Sometimes it's simple words and whether a person assumes that makes the biggest difference. I guess we all just need to keep talking, learning and listening. I really hope things improve, not only for me but for those to come. There's been a lot of pain for me and trauma physically and mentally; so much held in for so long.

However the last few years of speaking out have taught me that it wasn't for nothing. I'm helping others by simply sharing, I'm breaking the pattern for change.

You know the youth, they matter too!

Natasha Owens - POI at thirteen years old XXX

Natasha talks so vulnerably online about her journey, surgeries and symptoms, check her out on:

Instagram: @natashaowens1976

Rule 10   Enlighten Your Loved Ones

DO THE GUYS REALLY GET IT?

We've established this isn't just for the girls to know about...so talk to the boys too. The only difference in any conversations we should be having between any genders is simply the terminology of: **it will happen to you, or, it will happen around you.** When standing on London's Embankment with a massive board painted with 'Why aren't you talking about menopause?', my fellow Menovists and I were amazed just how many men came to chat to us and just how many were in their twenties and thirties. All willing to test their existing knowledge or learn more, sharing stories of their mums, colleagues and partners. They celebrated our efforts to raise awareness, confiding in us how those at home were really struggling. This filled me with such hope and joy.

It was when I shared my own experience, holding lengthy conversations with my own dad, that he acknowledged how little he knew about what my mum went through. How closed he'd been to learning at that time. Yet here he was, seen as a hardened generation at age seventy-seven, having these open chats and even gaining a new perspective. Whatever the age, this topic is worthy to be held and spoken aloud, and perhaps we should give more credit to the listening ears around us, that are possibly waiting for it unknowingly.

> **I realise now I just didn't ask about what your Mum was going through. I'm so glad we can chat now and feel privileged you talk to me about it, I really didn't know that menopause affected a person so much.**
>
> My Dad aged seventy-seven

Reflections

Rule 10   Enlighten Your Loved Ones

Hey I'm Sam...

We've Got to Talk

Fibroids and Endometriosis had me bleeding three weeks of every month, until I had my full hysterectomy. Prior to the op, the consultant told me stuff I really wanted to hear; I'd been in so much pain. I don't recall any conversations about the impact after and I'd not considered how this might feed into my relationship with my girlfriend. My GP mentioned HRT, but I elected not to have it. I was naive and thought I could manage it by myself thinking, 'I'm a fucking fierce woman. I can deal with this the natural way'. I remember being told as a child to, 'leave your mum alone...it's the change,' whatever the change was! She didn't talk about it and coming from Anguilla she is of a culture to crack on and deal, so I was doing the same.

I'd have Black Cohosh with Sage and Turmeric juices daily (it wasn't cheap) and after about eleven months my mood became irritable and short tempered. My poor girlfriend was dealing with her own hormonal changes, and I didn't treat her very well. Around her periods she'd be more sensitive, needing more from me which would heighten my irritability. I felt like such a bitch, with little patience and suddenly anything from spooning to just the feeling of warm breath would get on my nerves. I was intolerable. We talked about her periods but never linked back to my hormonal changes. I just didn't open up enough about how I felt like my personality was shifting. Sometimes it might seem easier to have those conversations between two women and we had talked about PMT before, sharing what each other might need, but I'd only ever mutter the words around my own menopause symptoms in my head. Two differing female hormonal changes happening at once was a difficult mix, because the communication didn't happen on my part. I only realise looking back that this probably contributed to our relationship not working.

SAME SEX COUPLES, IS IT DOUBLE TROUBLE?

Some of us might confide in our closest friends, those who are on the same page with symptoms or compare notes! But what if you're actually living with a woman going through this sharing the same bed? I thought about how this would feel for same sex couples, as the duvet on duvet off dance doubles in intensity or the changes in hormones duplicate throughout the relationship. Is it better, more understanding? Or worse as it's like a double whammy? I'm simply leaving these thoughts here. Just as a nod of openness for us all to think about how it might feel for other relationships to our own.

I think, particularly for lesbian couples where changes could happen together or hormones run wild, read all the books, listen to the podcasts and do the research. Talk about what you need, the things learnt and what you feel so you can manage it together. We can't always see it when we're in it, so your partner can look out for you and you for them too. I wish I had done more in finding out or asking the questions.

Although I'm fifty-four now and this is still part of my life, I did hang up the perceived badge of honour to 'get on with it' and took HRT. Easy breezy old Sam was back. It felt gentle again and the miserable Sam had gone. I felt like me again within three months, it was a blessed relief.

Sam Adams - Surgical menopause at forty-one years old XXX

Although Sam doesn't talk menopause online, she is a fierce life coach (she hates this term, calls it wanky!), trained in breathwork and founder of 'The Real Life Club'. She's bloody amazing! Find her at:

Website: sam-adams.com

Instagram: @samadamscoach

Dear Those Around Me....

Sometimes it's just too hard to say how we feel, so I've written this letter for you to share with the person/people you are closest with to read...if you think it will help.

To the dear person living with a menopausal warrior,

Firstly, I appreciate that you are reading this, and she will be thankful too.

I want you to know that she's doing her best as she tries to manage something that might not be fully understood yet, she's learning as she goes. This might drive you mad as much as it is her, the mood changes are volatile I know, from everything is rosy, to angry, sad and even the most terrifying rages...this isn't 'just her', it's the hormones creating a frenzy within the stories of her brain. She's tired, worried about things that may not have ever phased her confidence before, and there are times when her body doesn't feel her own. It aches, itches or the heat is so intense that she could faint and her mind is slower than her ideas. She's forgetful, I get it, but be patient, she's trying so hard to remember all the things. You may be questioning, 'where is the person I knew? She's asking herself that exact same question, feeling sometimes lost , but she's still there and one day will be so much more again.

She wants to feel sexy, to feel alive, yet her energy is low and her connection to that part of her seems distant. This is temporary, show you care, giving her space to reconnect with herself...you'll reap the benefits of understanding this, I promise. That once boldness may shrink while her body may gain, it's a battle she's fighting and to not feel beautiful in yourself is difficult, please don't add to her anguish...just hold acceptance and encouragement. A voice once loud may not feel able to speak up now; please support her with what is needed medically...go along to the doctors, share the fight.

Observe and listen maybe more than you did before. Ask her what she needs and express what you need too, you are just as important. It may seem like she loathes you, like she wants to escape you or others, maybe she does - fleetingly! But we all want to escape sometimes, it's often just to find ourselves.

She's in a cluster of symptoms and changes, I know it's also hard for you...seeing her like this, not knowing when you're right or wrong, sometimes just letting it be helps. But amongst all this there's a fire within her...I hope you're ready? Because she will step into something amazing, finding her new self and it may be different to before. Knowing what's worth her energy and what isn't, there'll be confidence and giving less hoots about pleasing people. Part of her service to others is knowing she has to serve herself first...you might find this tricky, or you may relish in watching her glow. This is her movement into her next chapter, like a goddess passing into a new realm. Show her you're by her side throughout, be curious to learn more, hold her when needed and walk away when a breath must be taken. Talk, share and talk some more...

You are the person she is showing this to. You're the person she loves enough to read these words, because some, if not all, will be what she is trying to say. She's sharing them with you because she wants you there with her. She just needs you to know what's happening, what she's feeling in those moments where it seems like she's lost her shit. She wants you to understand all of this because she trusts you the most.

Thanks for being that person for her...she's very lucky indeed

V x

Rule 10 Enlighten Your Loved Ones

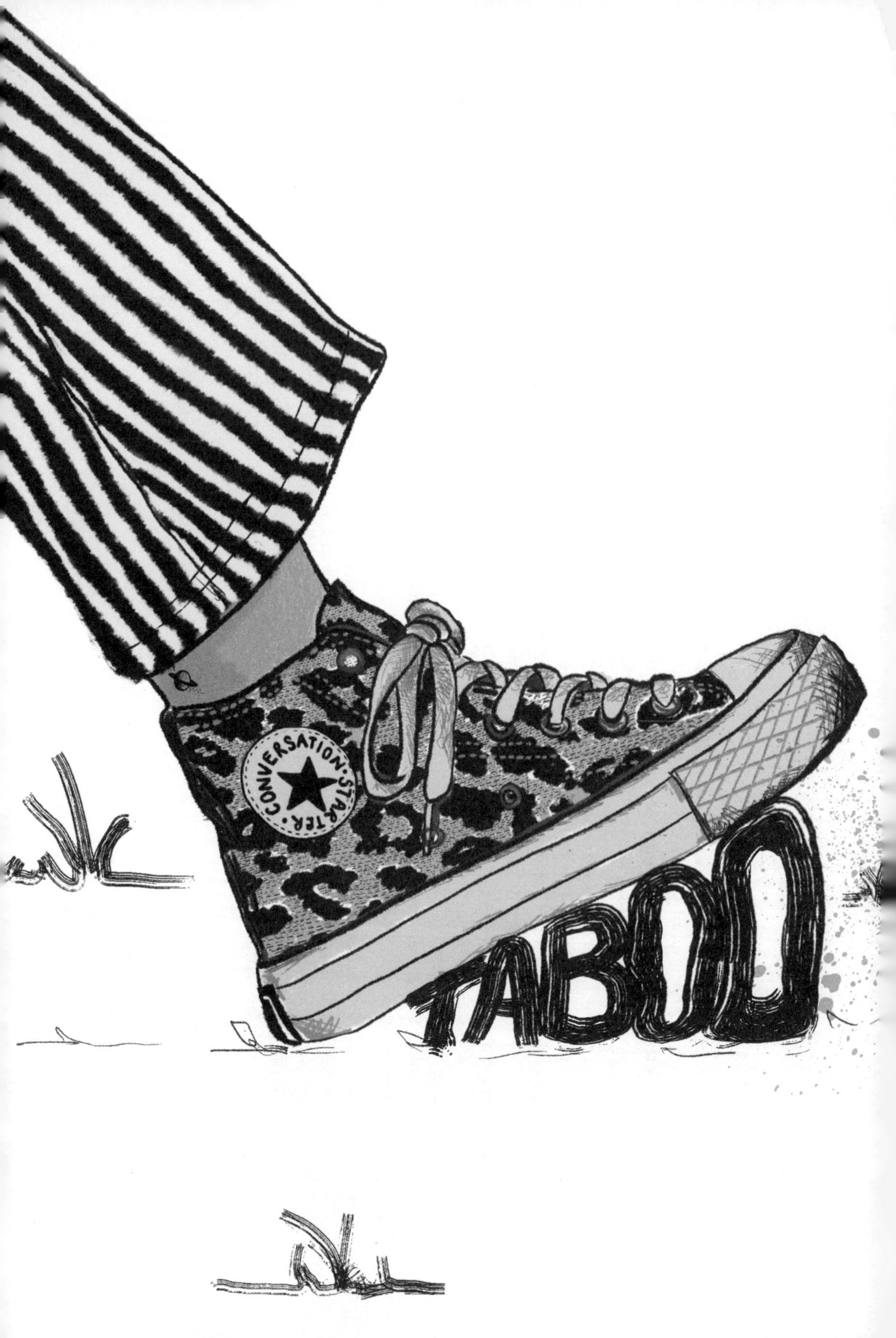
CONVERSATION STARTER
TABOO

11 RULE

Crushing THE TABOO IN Society

This has got to be one of the most important parts of this menopause conversation – the taboo of it all! We're slowly learning more about ourselves, how the healthcare system needs to change and we can see how history has impacted the way we think, but what's the next step? How do we change the narrative around this subject, not only for ourselves but for future generations to come? How do we totally and utterly crush the taboo? Because as our bodies manoeuvre, there is no getting away from menopause showing up in our everyday lives.

I like to disrupt the norm a bit and challenge thinking and it's amazing how not only the confident in voice can be the ones shouting for others who are less so, but also how those who feel they could never talk openly still make a huge impact in changing the dialogue too. I hope this section connects you to more experiences that you might not have thought about. These may even serve as conversation starters, but first it starts with your own experience.

When you arrived at that terminal for peri-menopause or menopause, or if you're getting your bags packed ready, how prepared were/are you for the flight? Jot down what you had/have been told and by whom:

How did this make you feel?

I want you to think about what you've written as you read on. Imagine someone else feeling the way you did/do and in whatever way feels right, lean in to how you can either amplify that, or change it for the better.

THE STIGMA WE CARRY

You might already have it down in sharing your menopause, on the right meds or longing to be so or now seeking the help you deserve. Maybe you're openly asking for alternatives if HRT is a no go for medical reasons. But for some of you, it's understandable that society has had an impact on how you view this time. What people will think, say or how they might treat you differently. Fear mixed with assumption, along with what has been before, somehow merges and it's an 'I'm okay, I'm going to just dredge through and hope for the best'.

I see many women, symptomatic, struggling, and yet there they are... wading through, knackered, not themselves, it's like they're wearing an invisible badge of honour handed down by generations with the sentiment of 'just get on with it'. Why are we doing that to ourselves... whhhhy? What for? For who? You simply don't have to. There's enough stigma around menopause, **it's time to stop placing that stigma upon ourselves...period!**

BADGE OF HONOUR

Lay down that badge of honour,
There's no need for it now,
No need to get by, suffer, crack on,
To just deal with how you feel,
This badge worn by so many,
Pinned over silent mouths,
Generations of fear, aching bodies, minds,
Let it fall, it's had its time,
May it rest there for a while,
Changing shape, words disappear
No help, I'm fine, no HRT
All muster to words of new,
A fresh badge worn with power,
For others to admire,
Acknowledgment, help, voices loud
Now spelling out,

My Rules!

Rule 11   Crushing The Taboo In Society

WORK WORK WORK!

Hold on to your pants, buckle up, we're diving into the place where statistically most crumple with the thought of talking openly about what's going on! We spend a huge proportion of our time working and yet in many stages throughout our lives, data shows this is the one place we don't always feel we can be our real selves, let alone when we're going through something seen as taboo or personal. Talking about this stuff at work is tough, it's no party and almost eighty per cent of women aren't comfortable to share symptoms with their manager. This is pretty rubbish and says a lot about our work cultures. Keeping it in dilutes our energy, rather than owning the reality of being human and sharing when things are not so great, enabling us to actually work towards a solution and show up rock solid when you are on your game.

This isn't easy I know, but **the reality is we're leaving work due to symptoms,** we're making excuses to avoid looking less capable, almost gaslighting ourselves as we sit at check outs, smile at reception desks, interrogate criminals and literally fight fires! We're apologising to the guys in meetings because we're suddenly sweaty, maybe turning a joke on ourselves, or because that peri-menopausal period has arrived without notice, and we slink off hidden and unheard. But who are we embarrassed for? Let me tell you, we're literally embarrassed for their embarrassment, and this is one of the things that stops us being seen for who we really are, a person.

I don't know why we do this, but it's getting us nowhere and the stats will continue to rise, amazing women will keep leaving during the peaks of their careers, the next generation of workforce will continue be muffled with a hush culture...unless we shed the embarrassment of others with a more it's 'not my monkey' approach.

And let me tell you something, it doesn't matter how many menopause policies are put in place, how many support groups, focus sessions or awareness days, **if we can't simply say what is happening in the moment to those we work closely with, then the culture won't really move forward.**

But what about the perception that being open and human is weak? Well, I call 'bullshit' to this! Everyone is a little broken, everyone goes through something, and it really has no hierarchy. The first thing I did when I returned to work after some time off was to share an email about why I couldn't work. I sent it out to everyone explaining that my mental health had got so low that I needed to take time to rest, recover and get well. The first thing I noticed was this allowed people to process that info in the workplace for themselves, not feeling awkward if they wanted to know more or support me finding my feet again. Next, I saw how full my inbox was with people opening up about themselves, colleagues I never thought would have ever sent me that email! I started to weave my surgical menopause symptoms into my day, by simply saying something like, 'I'll get back to you after my menopausal brain has reflected,' instead of trying to fire multiple ideas like I used to. I was setting clear expectations that 1) this is how I'll work for now, 2) you'll still get what you need, and 3) an explanation, and 4) I was going to talk about this stuff. Dropping in the odd symptom in the moment I was feeling them would help my team understand that things were changing for me, and as I was sat between the new kids on the block and the established CEOs, I can honestly say that on both sides they were learning.

The intention with that first ever email was merely to say, **'it's ok to be human'**, yet my small changes went on to big things at work. Eventually it brought an inclusive menopause conversation to a global audience, where CEOs talked openly about their own experiences and learns and colleagues messaged me about their struggling partners, asking what they could do…so you see, the honesty paid off. Not just because the culture of that place was slowly changing, but because through my own struggles, I could talk about my bad days, hatch a plan and adapt and overcome what would crop up. Managers do have a part to play here, alongside HR departments, wellbeing agendas, strategies and workplace adjustments, however small ripples make big waves and being freer with our speech can make the biggest difference in how we feel at work day to day.

I'm not saying I hit the gold at the end of the rainbow and quite honestly in some workplaces or teams you can't always polish a turd…but you can make tiny nudges with those around you count for your benefit. **You know you are kick-ass at work, you're just adjusting to something new. There is no shame in that.**

If you could say anything at work to make your life easier, what would you say?

What support groups are there in place? If none, how could you make one happen?

What resources can you share that will help your manager? These could be sent via email, asking them how they think they can support you. Their job is to help you remember!

Hello I'm Claire...

Flood In The Boardroom

Pre kids, pre serious career and those multiple divorces, when I had no real responsibilities and the only dilemmas I faced were food in my mouth, which lipstick shade and going out, I grasped every opportunity and flourished with no real thought for later life. My only real understanding of the older female generation was my mum and her friends. I remember the first time I heard her refer to someone as 'a woman of a certain age.' What is a 'woman of a certain age?' I thought. I couldn't get my head around it.

Well, thirty something years on and I'm now that woman! Grown up children, an all-consuming job and a renovation project that's just too big for one person! I also have confidence and a self-belief that comes with age and experience and for the most part I'm happy in my own skin. The biggest challenge of recent years however has definitely been peri-menopause. Not just what it's done to my body and emotions but how it's tested me on a practical level, in ways I never imagined. I'm not sure how I would have coped had I been experiencing this as the reckless nineteen-year-old I was.

Managing the ups and downs of peri-menopause and trying to maintain a consistent approach to work has been the hardest thing. I travel a lot with my job, working in a male-dominated industry, my colleagues are predominantly men in suits with serious titles and weighty responsibility and - whether my perception or a reality - being a 'woman of a certain age' going through peri-menopause just makes my work life that much harder.

Off I flew on a business trip, a week of back to back meetings around a boardroom table with a load of suits. My new HRT was now in the hand-luggage, having just been prescribed as I hadn't had a period for months. I walked in to my first meeting after a night of very little sleep, night sweats and stomach pains, sat down and within minutes I knew something wasn't right. Oh shit...on a pale upholstered meeting

WE ARE FLYING BY THE SEAT OF OUR SOMETIMES FLOODED PANTS... AND THAT'S OKAY.

chair, in my pale-coloured knotted dress…I felt the bloody world fall out of my back-side…literally. The horrible flooding feeling came from nowhere, but somehow (and I can't quite believe it) a calmness took hold. I just knew I had to get up and get out of that room. You couldn't write it. I stood up placing my large laptop bag behind my bottom, made my excuses and trotted through the door. To say confused faces swept around that table is an understatement.

After a trip to the pharmacy and a hastily tied jumper around my waist, I reappeared, feeling no need to explain myself! No-one dared look me in the eye or simply ask, 'Are you ok? Anything we can do?' I remember thinking, these men have wives, daughters, sisters, they must have experienced this in some way before and if they hadn't…ha, they have now! I wasn't embarrassed, I just felt physically uncomfortable. I thought wow if you can do this, carry on and bring yourself back to focusing on your work, you are amazing!' I was proud of myself.

Back in the UK, I told Mum. She recounted a similar experience many years ago when out shopping with my dad. They hurried back to the car, drove home and she went to bed. For her it was traumatic, a shameful experience and one that still causes her anxiety when she recalls it. For me it was liberating, slightly awkward but liberating. It just goes to show 'women of a certain age' means something different now. I wear that badge with pride. Part of this phase is being menopausal. Yes, it's challenging and some days I long for those carefree teenage years, but it's easier for me than it was for Mum. It's not so taboo or shameful and I can talk about it and, more importantly, I have the strength to step into it and not hide away.

Claire Williams - Peri-menopause at age fifty-one XXX

BOSSING IT ALONE

Let's not forget that during and after menopause we're more likely to have entrepreneurial thoughts, we're ignited, creative and stepping into roles such as leadership with more empathy and drive. We shouldn't dismiss that some choose to leave a career because they see a better way. So, what if you're self-employed, who looks after you then? With no HR in your corner, you have to be it all. What comes with this is the freedom to just be yourself on your own terms, but equally there's difficulty in cutting yourself a break, or setting up your own support system for when you need it.

What things do you have in place if you're self-employed to support yourself through this time? (Think mentally, physically, support network)

Rule 11 Crushing The Taboo In Society

WHAT IF I'M STUDYING?

I can't deny there will be a stark difference here, purely because although it may not be talked about at work so openly yet, there is a still a murmur that a proportion of a workforce will be experiencing this change. When you're at college or uni possibly the last thing your lecturers or tutors will be thinking is that one of their students are going through menopause.

Start by seeing what well-being support is available to you, this may include any counselling services which most education facilities have. This will be your first step to starting the conversation. If you're not too comfortable chatting to the staff you have a good rapport with, perhaps try an email linking some helpful information on POI for example and how this shows up. Accompany this with how it could affect your studies around your symptoms, and throw the question back to them about how they think they could support you? Remember, they're teachers...they have a thirst for learning and will welcome your shared vulnerability, they'll relish in learning something themselves that will add another string to their bow of caring for their students.

Write down anything you would like to draft in your email, or points you want to get across:

Rule 11   Crushing The Taboo In Society

Hi I'm Sheree...

From A Child In Menopause To A Woman With A Mission

If I could turn back time and tell my younger self anything it would be:

Sheree, it's okay to have bad days, these will help you appreciate the good and be kinder to yourself. Know your worth. Don't worry that you look different or feel different from others, the world is far bigger than you think, and your worries aren't as massive as they may seem. Just be you! From adolescent Menopause to a young woman on a mission, be bold, speak out and research the unknown.

Look at you, you are doing it...you have purpose.

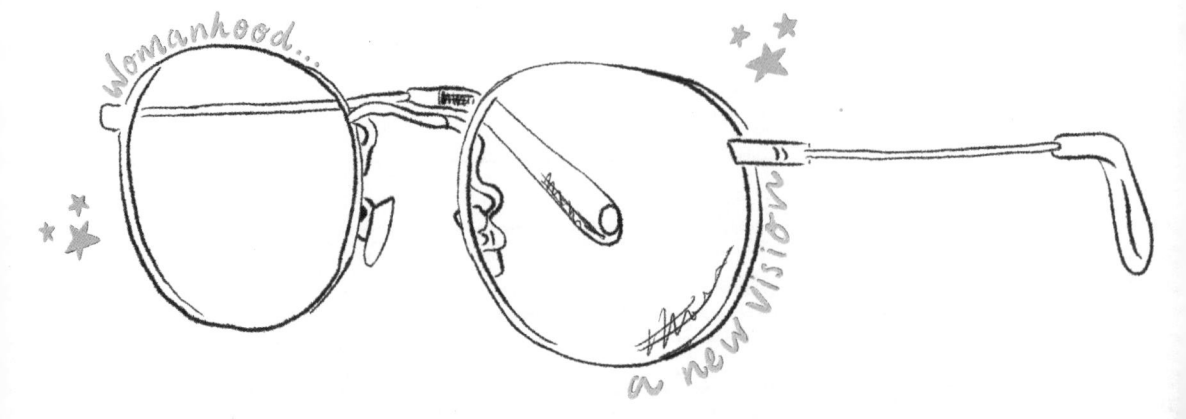

I wish I was taught about what it means to be a woman because I always thought that womanhood meant motherhood and to be a mother is the only way to truly be a woman. I now know that the two do not equate and that I am in fact a wonderful woman!

Sheree Hargreaves XXX POI from age seven

This girl! She is paving the way to educate and advocate for POI, her personality is simply infectious. Sheree can be found on:

Instagram: @lifeofpoi_

For What Was Before

In grief there is the sense,
That we'll never be the same,
A love for what was had,
Or what there could have been,
For who we were before,
Or who others hoped we'd be,
Why would we stay still,
When circumstances change?
You are allowed to grieve,
For whatever you feel you've lost,
You are allowed to feel those things,
Soak them in, make peace,
As over you they wash.

allow the grief to come

Rule 11   Crushing The Taboo In Society

YOU ARE ALLOWED TO GRIEVE

Grief in itself is a societal taboo. It can sometimes feel like we welcome it, without really acknowledging fully all the aspects of loss; it's like we don't quite know what to do with it. Whether we are pushing it down or changing how we react to someone else's, it's important that amongst the shenanigans of this change we give grief the space it deserves. You might be feeling a sense of loss for a whole host of reasons around what's happening to you. Grieving this is valid and you are allowed to feel whatever it is you are feeling. I don't have to name the reasons why you feel what you do at this time, or name what's either lapping at your feet, or coming over you in a tidal wave...

I will simply give you space to write whatever you need if it helps...

Czesc Michel...

Not Just a Woman's Problem! –

I chatted to a colleague, Michel Deronzki, a trans man who experienced symptoms throughout his transition in his twenties. He told me about how he had to find his way through a mix of physical surgical changes and societal acceptance, all whilst battling low mood, loneliness and feeling so angry about the smallest of things. He would also get severe hot flushes, where he would wear next to nothing in the icy Polish temperatures where he lived. We talked about how his mum was his grounding voice and how he too had to juggle his dosage of HRT to get things right. Michel's aim was to reduce the Estrogen in his body and increase Testosterone, the side effects can be any of those symptoms listed at the top of this book.

He, like me, had been to a darker place and it was joyous to see him light up as he spoke about the support of his friends and how he was now settled, had a great job and was finally who he was meant to be. I realised our differing gender and menopause didn't matter as we compared notes and similarities. Like myself he was so dependent on good support and the right hormones – we'd felt the same. It was a chat I'll never forget; it opened my eyes and I hope to pass that on.

I'm so glad people are open to learn more about what it means to transition and the effects of HRT in terms of symptoms for someone like me.

Michel Deronski   Trans menopause aged twenty-nine   XXX

> 'Sisterhood is holding space for one another to be our full selves - whatever that looks like. Messy or not. It's loving each other while we figure life out.'
>
> Ashley Hobbs

Hey I'm Mabel

Trans And No Testosterone

I've now had full top and downstairs surgery, so I have a vagina and vulva and I'm very proud of my lady bits, but of course I've also experienced the battles with HRT and the first year was absolute hell. When taking Estrogen to feminise, the most horrendous mood swings were the biggest side effect. I find the more I take the more volatile my moods are; the higher the highs, the lower the lows, but I'm used to it now, although it's taken a while for it to stabilise. But because I've had the downstairs surgery, I don't naturally produce any Testosterone at all, and it's just as important for me now as it is in anyone's hormonal regime. This helps my energy and libido, so I would definitely recommend it to any woman to help them feel more motivated. I remember not being able to get out of bed without it!

Mabel Clifton - Trans menopause aged thirty-one XXX

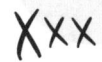

TRANSGENDER MENOPAUSE

'What do you mean it has no gender? Ridiculous!' is a fair representation of some of the comments I get when I post online about menopause not just being about women! I'm not de-feminising what is happening here, I'm merely being inclusive that the experience of menopausal symptoms is not just felt by cis-women. Gender and our sex are, of course, two very different things. Our sex assigned at birth doesn't always represent the gender that we identify as, it's quite simple really. Whether gender fluid, non-binary or transgender, you too may have either biological, surgical or chemically induced menopause. You too may or may not take HRT or feel all the feels of the symptoms, and your voice in society around menopause care is even smaller than mine, which makes me incredibly sad.

Introducing My Dear Neighbour Pauline

Post Menopause

In a cosy front room, cuppa in hand, I sensed we were both a little nervous. I call her 'Lady Pauline' as she is a Queen at eighty-two, with a cheeky spark in her eye and a huge heart full of love for us as her family next door. Yet I was conscious of going too far, stepping over the edge of her privacy.

'I've just been out for lunch with the girls,' she said.

This is a good place to start, I thought.

'So do you talk, or did you ever chat about the menopause with the girls?' Straight in I went…

Pauline told me how it really wasn't spoken about, apart from the odd comment on hot flushes. 'We just sort of got on with it…like my Mum too, we weren't prepared, we didn't talk about things back then. It was deemed as private…you'd never ask your Mum!' Her eyes almost filling with surprise, reflecting on how things have changed. Her face relaxing, she recalled a time where her mum's mood swings had her chasing her sister down the garden path!

'My sister would run towards the bathroom,' Pauline sang, slightly giggling, 'which was the only room in the house with a lock!'

I asked, 'So what about you? Do you remember any symptoms?' taking another sip of tea.

'Hot flushes mainly, oh and night sweats, they were just awful,' she said, sharing when her late husband Reg would make jokes about the duvet tog and that she'd wake him up! 'I still have these sometimes now,' she said. 'I'm a terrible sleeper, it never really went, come to think of it.'

We talked about how for her and her friends symptoms went on well beyond the time when menopause would have been deemed to be over. I could see her reflecting, maybe this conversation was connecting dots for Pauline in real time?

'Thinking about it, Mum had these terrible headaches too. She'd take herself off,' she paused…'I had them too, this would have been the time of my menopause, because as soon as it went so did they.'

I scribbled my notes and just listened, I could feel that she too was learning as much as me at this point.

'I'd go off to a room, the kids were little…my son answered the phone once because I couldn't, telling whoever it was I was in the room in the dark…he must have only been about four!' she laughed.

'What about HRT, was that something you took?' I was keen to see how the experience of medical care was different to now.

'Hmmm well, I definitely took pills…no clue what they were! The doctor just said I was going through menopause and to take them…handing me the note.'

We chatted about my experience in surgical menopause: how it had rocked my mental health, how the medical system isn't set up to support all kinds of menopause, voluntary GP modules and the lack of research in woman's health and HRT, sharing a disbelief that in the current decade this was the case! I watched the surprise flow over Pauline's kind face as I spoke statistics of those leaving work, how the near eighty symptoms weave their way through the varying experiences of gender, age and culture.

Two women, two generations apart…both holding space to listen and learn from each other in this moment of openness. Pauline talked of a healthcare system before large GP clinics, where nurses would visit the home and time, along with a nice cup of tea, would be given. I sensed that they may not have talked openly about private health matters out in the community, yet in a way woman still felt supported. I scribbled my last notes, swallowed down the last of my cuppa and thanked Pauline for the chat.

'Safe journey home,' she joked as I made my way to the other side of the driveway. I was filled with a sense of connection, no list of endless symptoms or struggles from a generation that had been before, but a sense that, again, menopause was and is, just as it is. That however unique the experiences, it brings us together and this chat had done that in so many ways.

Rule 11   Crushing The Taboo In Society

MANOPAUSE

Did you know men can experience menopausal symptoms too? I know, I know... feminists be upstanding! I'm just giving this a little bit of space, it's my empathetic side coming out. Known as the **Andropause** (male menopause) or labelled as the manopause, it's a time when male bodies change and hormones fluctuate too. Usually around fifty, because the testosterone levels drop.

Some of the symptoms include:

- ✓ Mood swings and irritability
- ✓ Loss of muscle mass, reduced ability to exercise
- ✓ Fat re-distribution. Think larger bellies and man boobs
- ✓ Lack of enthusiasm
- ✓ Difficulty sleeping
- ✓ Short term memory loss

I'm just placing this here because maybe we have more in common than we think, which might just bring people together in talking more, about how this stuff seeps into our everyday lives and relationships with each other.

Okay, back to us!

DIFFERENT CULTURES

It doesn't matter what country you live in or our cultural differences, over half of the world's population will go through this. What does make a difference is how our cultural communities and countries react or support. For example, in a lot of Asian cultures menopause is not recognised. There is no word for it in certain languages, whereas in China it is classed as a profound and wonderful time. They believe that the energy that was needed in the uterus moves up to the heart and spills out in wisdom to teach the next generation – how beautiful is that? There are even differences between how symptoms are experienced between the eastern and western world. However communities *are* coming together, new generations of aunties and sisters within families are starting to share symptoms and stories, so we need to hold space for this.

As much as I've asked you to be curious about yourself, **be curious about other cultures too.** I'm still learning along with you. Don't be afraid to ask how it is for another, what are the differences, the similarities? Learn, connect and help each other to feel more comfortable, this helps squash the societal boundaries that can sometimes be placed around us.

Rule 11   Crushing The Taboo In Society

Hi I'm Faye...

Going It Solo And Changing Cultural Stigma

My journey has definitely been a solo one in every which way! I was the first of my girl group to have symptoms...so there was no going to them for advice. I was forty-five, single, still going out and having fun. I actually laughed when I had my first hot flush as I thought, 'nah this can't be happening to me, this happens to old ladies with white hair.'

Although many women are frightened by menopause and the associated idea of getting older, that didn't even cross my mind. It was, however, a surprising taboo and as the hot flushes came, what I noticed was I feared talking about it a work. No-one seemed to be having the conversation, let alone any black women, and when looking for advice there was none. I was curious to know if my symptoms would be different from white women. I slowly told friends and family, but it was only after starting my own menopause project that I opened up to colleagues.

As I edged closer to peri-menopause, I noticed how assumptions in society became amplified. People presuming I had kids or that I was part of a couple. My heart would tug. I'd find myself feeling annoyed; I very much wanted children, but it was not to be. It was a time of acknowledging this wasn't going to happen for me and making peace with myself, then peri-menopause drops in my lap. I was trying to work out my symptoms, my feelings, whilst hearing, 'How old are your kids?' 'Is your husband supportive?' One woman even said to me, 'But the menopause is easier for black women.' I was so shocked I couldn't even respond!

I was intrigued, and found that statistics were starting to show (in some cases) black women suffer worse symptoms and realising these women weren't speaking up and were navigating menopause whilst staying silent, mouthing 'we are fine,' when we weren't. I decided that had to change.

As I embarked on research my world suddenly imploded; the job became super busy and my mum was diagnosed with terminal cancer. Mum had me when she was seventeen and we were super close. These stressors increased my symptoms and I felt I was falling off a cliff. Insomnia and anxiety were the worst, whirling with hot flushes, brain fog, losing my hair and anger. It was a potent mix and I was on the floor!

I started to see a therapist for my anxiety and to help me come to terms with the fact that Mum was going to die. She advised me to see my GP, so I made an appointment. I'd heard stories of many women going to their doctors for menopause help and having been poo poo'd and sent away. I sobbed as I explained what I was feeling, and I thank my lucky stars that she listened! She suggested some blood tests, along with prescribing me HRT to help. I was only a year into my peri-menopause and had never thought of HRT. I'm more a holistic, homeopathic kinda person, yet here I was taking the help with both hands. I was desperate and this was one of the best things I've ever done. The first prescription (tablet) didn't feel right for me, but with patience I learnt there are various types of oral Estrogen and many different forms of HRT. Today I have the Mirena coil and use Oestrogel, it's the best I've ever felt.

Along with realising that black women stay quiet about menopause, they also definitely do not entertain HRT! It's like they're getting on with it, at a huge detriment to themselves. Very slowly I'm starting to see this change, but it's like they'd sooner suffer (and I mean suffer) than take it. Is that a systemic cultural thing? I thought.

Well, I say, 'Hell no to that! Why live a miser when you can get help and be so much more?'

Fay Reid - Peri-menopause at forty-five XXX

Fay is a massive advocate for menopause and shouts loud to advocate for women's cancer. She works with individuals and companies sharing her own experience as a woman of colour.

Website: fayreid.com

Instagram: 9to5menopause

WE'RE ALL BUILT DIFFERENTLY

When we see the world of menopause media around us, it all feels a bit similar. Age, female, able-bodied even status or celebrity. Don't get me wrong, any awareness is marvellous, but I can't help thinking what about those that are unseen? Those with learning difficulties, disabilities, those that are caring for them, and I thought how on earth must they be getting on? What if you're less able to do the things we often say are the easy stuff? The mindful walks, hitting the gym or even accessing the information needed in an accessible way? What if you're Autistic and sensory aspects are heightened? Or your ADHD/ADD is amplified with brain fog or fatigue for example. What if your body is changing in peri-menopause/menopause, but your mind just doesn't process to the age you are?

I chatted to a dad of a peri-menopausal lady with Down-Syndrome... her mental age was around ten years old. He was trying desperately to support his daughter Gemma whilst having to learn about menopause himself. His wife had passed away and he was doing it alone. He told me how his mother had been really honest with him as a boy about periods and he'd often go to the shop for her to buy the products she'd need. This was the start of moving the embarrassment aside around women's health, and he credited this to why he felt able to ask questions and join support groups now, to help with this stage in Gemma's life that he may not had thought to plan for.

He would explain to Gemma in a very matter of fact way what was happening, preparing for irregular unexpected periods and was learning to manage her mood changes but it was clear it was hard for them both. I really was in awe of our conversation as Gemma sat beside him showing me all the crafts she'd made. This was a guy who had to step up and he represented the people we often don't consider when we talk about this topic.

I can't pretend I have the answers, especially when thinking about access to proper support and healthcare in the current times. Even writing this book, I'm not sure it'll be accessible to everyone. What I can do, is consider this and create ideas, along with remaining open and curious about how menopause shows up for all, and I simply ask you to do the same.

But I want you to know, if you're feeling underrepresented, unheard, unseen? I hear you...I see you.

THERE ARE THOSE NOT LIVING WITH DISABILITY AND THERE ARE THOSE THAT ARE – MENOPAUSE TOUCHES US ALL.

Hello I'm Kerry...

My Experience Will Not Define Me

I sat with the forms in my hands, pen ready to squiggle my signature, about to under-go my full body Chemotherapy and Radiotherapy treatment. I had Leukaemia at fourteen and five years on was given the celebratory, 'all clear'. Just five months after that however I relapsed and now needed a stem cell transplant (courtesy of my brother). Here I was, about to undergo this evasive treatment to eradicate my own bone marrow so I could accept his. I was twenty-one.

Reading down the list of side effects: nausea, hair loss, problems eating…infertility…wait what? This was the first time I was seeing this word. In seconds I'd gone from tackling this next stage of trying to live, to processing a life that hadn't occurred to me, which may be very different to the one I'd planned living for.

There were never conversations about infertility, chemical menopause or POI before or after my treatment. Just, 'Here's some Estrogen HRT,' with no further explanation, no Testosterone and no emotional support. I was left for fifteen years (some of which at risk of stroke and blot clots), just me getting on with it. My friends and family were amazing, but even now I don't feel so comfortable talking about the true depths of infertility and what menopause after cancer feels like, but I'll get there. The constant, 'do you have any children?' questions from those not close, like it's the 'go to' for me to be a woman, are hard and I didn't feel I could just offload the whole story by the coffee machine at work! I became more and more withdrawn, and the next battle was around the corner.

The steroids from my cancer resulted in me developing Avascular Necrosis; the blood supply wasn't reaching my bones causing them to break down and die. I found myself in a wheelchair not able to stand or walk for twelve long years. Shortly after the joys of my wedding, I became depressed and anxious with no help managing this disjointed life and my Menopause symptoms. I thought, 'I can't do this anymore'. I knew I needed to do something, however I had no idea how life changing it would be.

Link in to your own strength

Searching online I found a small women's only gym, so I made a call. Explaining everything: how I couldn't walk, even lift my arm, let alone lift anything like kettlebells or weights, they welcomed me and literally had my back. I started small, just the machines with no extra weight and a lot of guidance, the months rolled as I slowly built more strength and made small changes. Over time I went from the shell of the person I'd been, to not only working out regularly but volunteering for a program to work there. My confidence grew and my empathy, listening ears and own experience seeped into charity projects helping others. I had wanted a better life and I was getting 'me' back, learning my capabilities now and how to advocate more, not taking 'no' for an answer.

If things in your life aren't feeling right...change them, making note of that little spark within. Take that first step - despite the disabilities, reframe the message.

I really hope for the future that Infertility and menopause support/information is available and in motion before and after someone has cancer treatment. Understand the big changes, be 'in the know' and don't suffer with your symptoms. Advocate for the life you deserve to have lived for.

Kerry Cameron - Chemical menopause at age twenty-one XXX

INTERVAL OF EVENTS

Ten months, endless voicemails, six hours waiting for an appointment where the consultant never showed, more voicemails and finally another date worth noting. I've taken a two-hour drive in a monsoon and I'm here crying. The implant is in!

Thirty minutes, two little stitches and hopefully this will give me the Estrogen boost I need. Tears of joy mixed with exhaustion are streaming, I feel relieved yet empowered all at once and hear myself say, 'watch out world!'

I hope it works, but my goodness it feels good to be at the end of this fight to feel better. I've learnt so much: that HRT isn't the only answer, choosing when to raise our voice along with learning when to step back, allows us to conserve the energy we need. In the end I chose to trust that eventually things will be ok, all whilst understanding how powerful we can be when faced with adversity.

Rule 11 Crushing The Taboo In Society

WE ARE PEOPLE NOT STATISTICS
CRUSH THE TABOO
SHOUT LOUD
IT HAS NO AGE!
"CHANGING THE FACES OF MENOPAUSE"
MENOPAUSAL and BADASS!
Advocate
Queen
Not GAME OVER!
#NOTJUSTAHASHTAG
#
FIERCE AF
RAGING HORMONES
F*CK MENOPAUSE

RULE 12

Create Change

FOR US, AND THE GENERATIONS TO COME

Whatever you took from the last two rules, the boldness to go out and shout loud, or quietly, and surely mention the odd thing within your home...you will make a difference. You will feel a little lighter and in your own way you'll be making an impact on the generations around you. The conversations may flow or be slower in pace...but you're still moving it forward and the ripples will travel further than you think. With doctors starting to be more educated and schools adding this to the curriculum, time is needed to let this stuff embed, but we should never underestimate the force that is the collective voice. If in our own ways we *all* speak a little more, we really can be the ones to bridge that gap.

Hello I'm Diane...

Raise Your Voice to #MakeMenopauseMatter

When personal experience makes you acutely aware of an unchallenged injustice that is affecting so many, you simply can't ignore it. The past few years of my life would have been much easier if I had ignored it, but I simply couldn't. Being catapulted into surgical menopause without the right information and support took me to the edge and very nearly claimed my life. I was fortunate to have someone in my life who took action in that moment, getting me that help and support when I couldn't do it for myself. BUT it should never have come to that.

Once feeling a little better, I wondered if it was just me who had been unlucky, however after a few hours researching online I discovered thousands of women also suffering in silence. I promised myself, if I ever felt like me again, I would make sure that I did something to change the menopause landscape for the future.

Two years later I launched menopausesupport.co.uk swiftly followed by the national #MakeMenopauseMatter campaign with four main aims:

- 1. Mandatory menopause training for all GPs and medical students.
- 2. Awareness and support in every workplace.
- 3. Menopause to be included in the RSE curriculum in schools.

4. A national government funded public health campaign for menopause.

I had absolutely no experience of activism or of campaigning, just a drive and priority for change, whatever it took. It can feel hard to speak publicly about a subject that's still taboo, and menopause was certainly still that in 2015 when I first shared my own experience on national TV. Things are very different years later, those in the public eye speaking up and the media taking a much greater interest. Awareness is improving all the time but the fundamental changes to menopause healthcare and support for all are still very much, work in progress.

As I write this, I'm delighted that we've achieved some of our campaign aims: having menopause added to the school curriculum in September 2020 and mandatory menopause training for all medical students will become a reality in 2024. We're heading in a positive direction with improving menopause support in some workplaces, so the focus now steers to all businesses to step up and for every current GP and practice nurse to experience mandatory menopause education. A national government funded awareness campaign is vital to ensure improved information and awareness for everybody.

Approximately half of the world's population will experience menopause directly. The other half will know or love someone who experiences it, so they're indirectly affected. My experience of supporting thousands of women is, without the right information, advice and support, menopause can affect their health and wellbeing, their relationships and their careers. For every one in four having very few symptoms, there is one in four describing theirs as debilitating, severely affecting their quality of life.

Surely, everyone deserves free help and support at the time they need it? If you find yourself agreeing, please, raise your voice too, by signing and then sharing the #MakeMenopauseMatter campaign with everyone you know. This ensures we will be the generation who can say…'we made menopause matter'.

Thank you.

Diane Danzebrink - Surgical menopause at age forty-five XXX

Public speaker, educator, wellbeing consultant and the founder of menopausesupport.co.uk and the national #MakeMenopauseMatter campaign. Diane is off the charts!

Website: menopausesupport.co.uk
Instagram: @dianedanzebrink

Please support the campaign by visiting change.org and searching for **'Make menopause matter'**.

PLAN OF ATTACK

I'd love you to think about what you wrote before about how you felt/feel going into menopause, what you knew/know and how the messages either reached you or passed you by. How can you change or build on that for others?

I raise my voice – not so that I shout, but so that those without a voice can be heard.

Malala Yousafzai

Rule 12   Create Change

MY PLAN OF ATTACK! WHAT THINGS COULD I DO TO CREATE CHANGE?

Remember there is strength in numbers and what most people have shared through the stories you've read have been finding their community. So, if that's your jam and you want to stand together with another kick-ass menopausal warrior…go find your people, they're out there waiting!

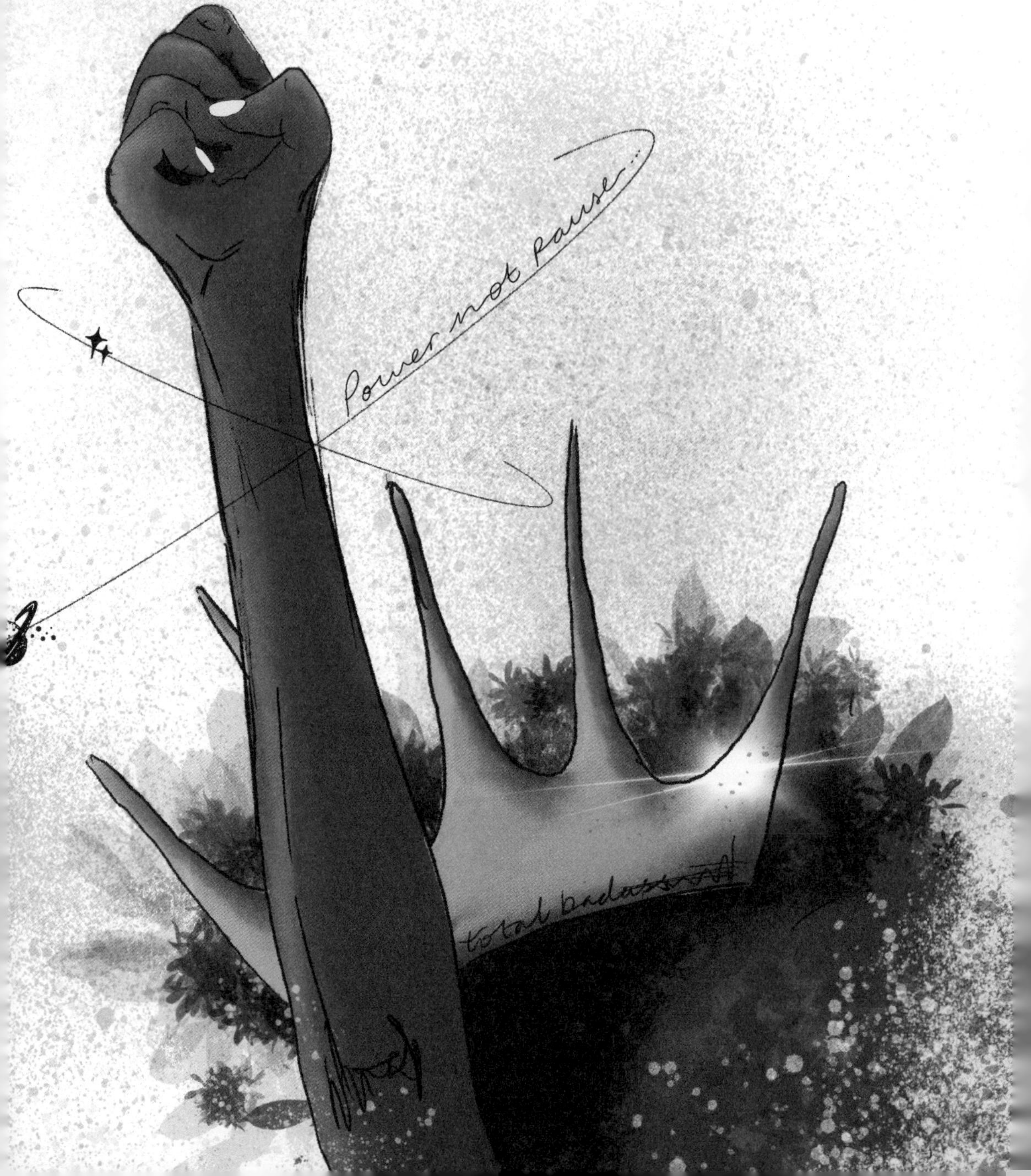
Power not pause...
total badass

THE ULTIMATE RULE

Always Remember, you're a Badass Queen!

Shakespeare once said...

'Though she be but little, she is fierce' and this could not be more true of this final tiny chapter.

These few but mighty pages are not only where you reach the end (jeez it was big, so take a bow) of this book, which I hope has served you as a companion of sorts, but is where you embark on your next adventure in leaning in even more to yourself.

As you turned each page to explore, together we have delved deep, been curious, thoughts have risen and you like me have made your own decisions that perhaps you didn't expect, or believed you couldn't or wouldn't have done before.

We're all still learning, about ourselves, our health, our wellbeing and what's expected of us at this time; the world will continue to turn outside, information will change, as will we, and there may always be a fight for what should be...

But that is the ride of being beautifully human, to find the quality of it all for ourselves, feeling the spectacular within the madness and the party in the mundane,

It's down to us to make ours, and you my friend are on your way...

So, that being said - I've one last thing I'd love you to do!

HOMECOMING WARRIORS

As our bodies change,
The balance is tilted,
We feel off centre,
But our souls are stirring,
We sit in the fire,
Unsure of the answers,
Minds start to ponder,
But our souls are awakening,
Fog sometimes heavy,
Thickness of purpose,
Tired in panic,
But our souls are lifting,
Like a Queen in training,
Letting go and accepting,
Stepping into the new,
Our souls are aligning,
Transitioning like warriors,
Wisdom and strength,
Not 'past it' or 'old',
Our souls now nourished,
No 'pause' but power,
We connect to ourselves,
That passage complete,
Our souls are now light,
Removing our armour,
Refreshed and rebalanced,
Our soul now ready,
To wear its crown.

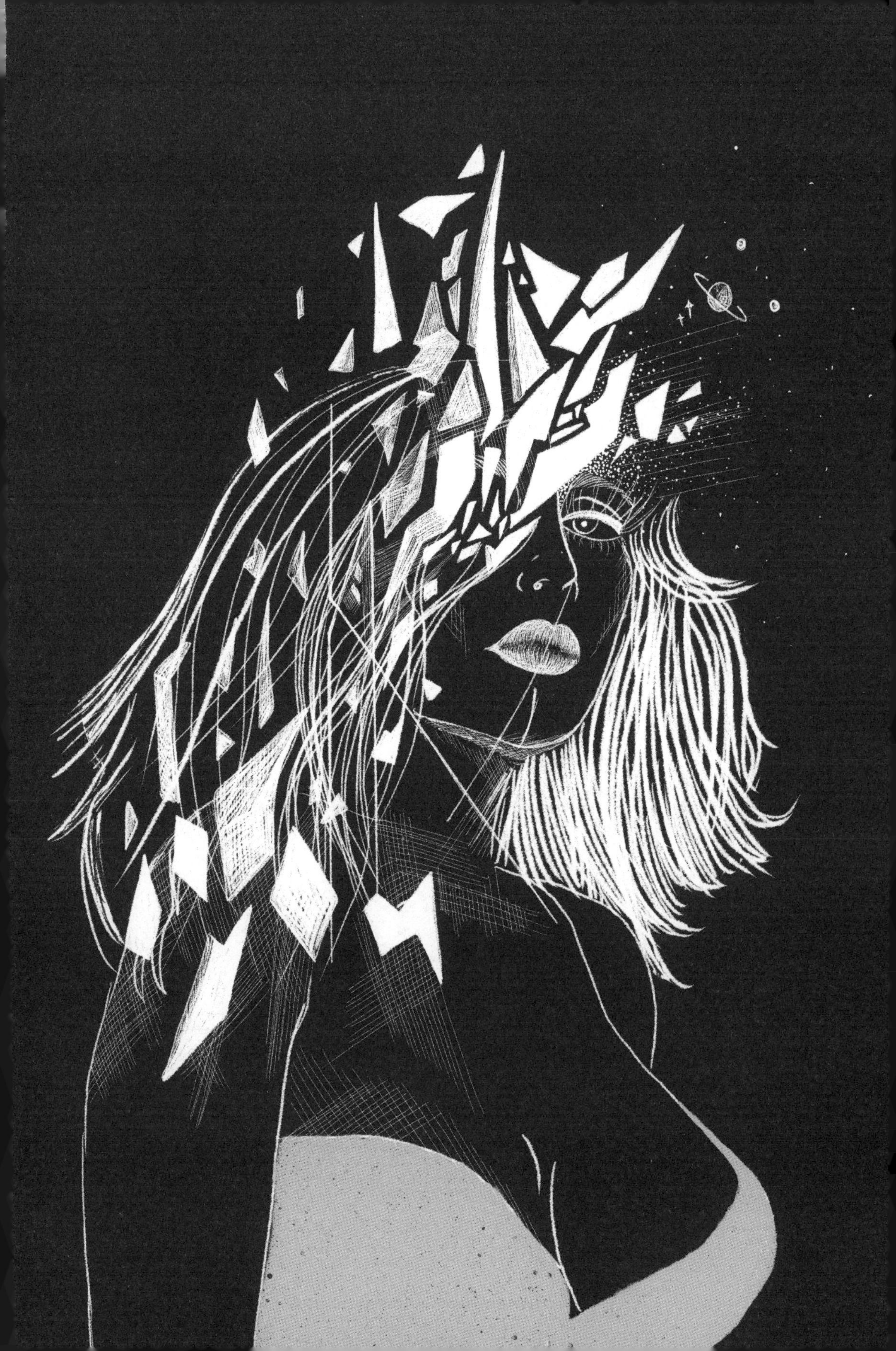

LETTER TO YOURSELF

I'm going to ask you to write a letter to yourself...yep!

Write how you're feeling, what you've accomplished, your highs, your lows, celebrations, losses, just wherever you are now. Whatever flows from your pen. It is yours to read in a year's time and simply reflect on the journey you are taking. Set a reminder to come back here in 12 months from this date and just see how far you'll have come.

It's a rather beautiful gift to yourself.

The Ultimate Rule   Always Remember You're a Badass Queen!

IT'S BEEN FUN...WELL I HOPE YOU THINK SO

I'd love you to look back to the beginning of this book and read the words you wrote as to why you chose to pick it up. How do you feel about them now? Take a moment to sit with that.

Whilst writing this book, I felt every thought deeply, reliving past experiences, whilst inhaling and exhaling the present too. As pen took to words and each sketch was inked, I felt like I was finding myself too, having to be brave, trying the unknown and swallowing down the doubt. It was a bold move to invest in myself in this way. Harnessing my own rules, aligning menopause as it is for me, with a sense of my own belonging, so I could come home to myself.

I hope you are carrying something within you now, that wasn't there before. Feeling somewhat ready to be the incredible menopausal warrior that you are, or that you may become when the time comes.

You may have submersed yourself in all I've asked, learning what's for you and what is not, you might have disagreed with me at times, even debated parts of this book in your own mind or with others...I really hope so! I hope there is a fierceness within yourself, in what's to come and hope we can be fierce yet kind to each other. I have no doubt you are well on your way to absolutely owning the shit out of your own menopause, defining your own rules as you go along,

So I'll leave you with this...

Be the light...step into who you are,
Because no-one belongs there more than you,
Own your mess, share the mistakes,
Keep learning, lean in,
Growing in love for yourself,
Just in the moment, that is now,
And you'll do fine.

I think you're ready to wear your kick ass Crown... Queen!

The Ultimate Rule　　Always Remember You're a Badass Queen!

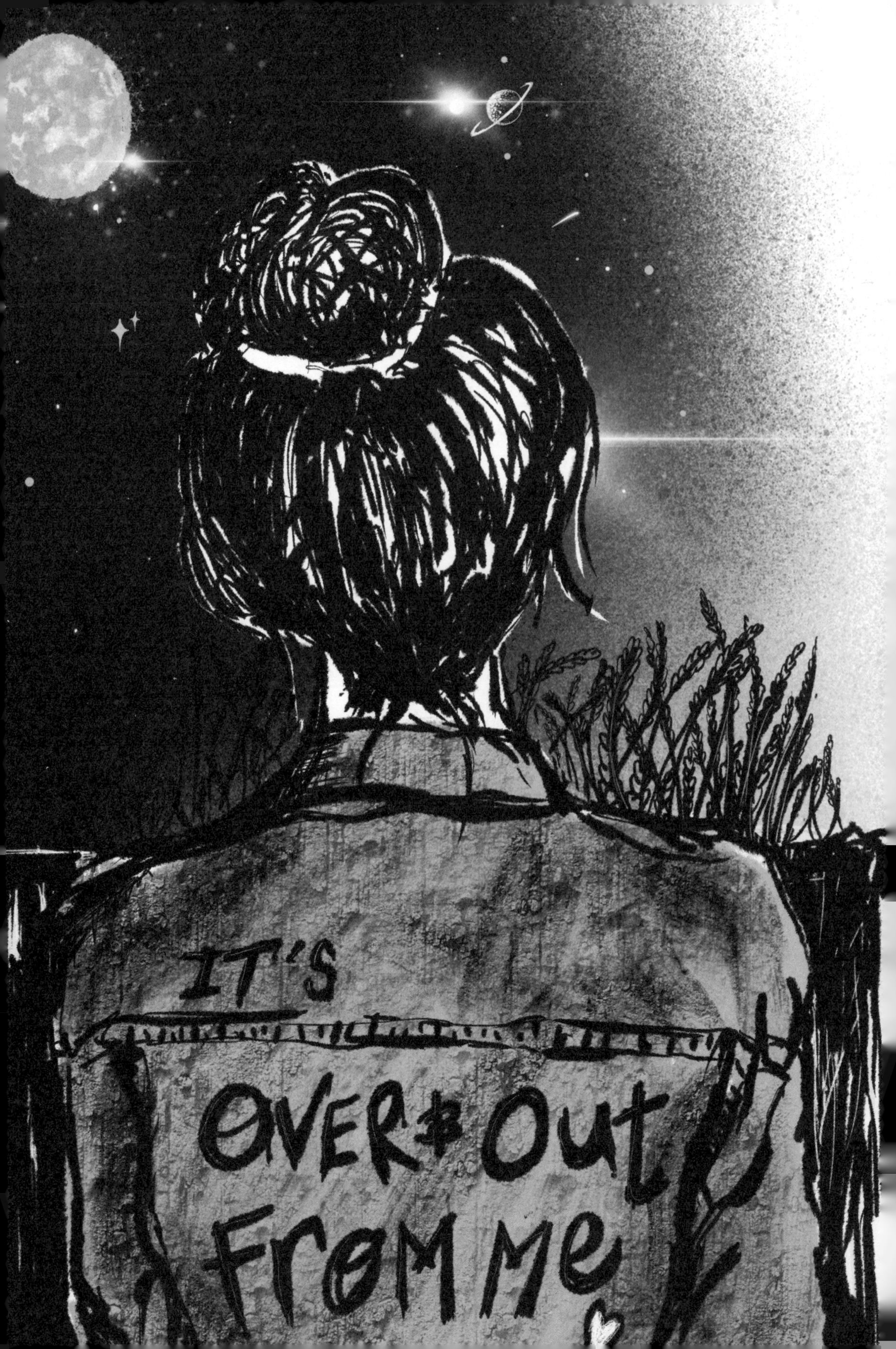
IT'S
OVER & OUT
FROM ME.

The little

LITTLE Exxtras

EXTRAS

THINGS THAT HELPED ME CHARITIES/SUPPORT

		🌐	📷	f	☎
CoppaFeel	Charity supporting breast cancer	coppafeel.org	@coppafeelpeople		
Menopause Matters	Full of up to date facts/support forums	menopausematters.co.uk	@menopausematters	Menopause Matters	
Mind	Mental health support	mind.org.uk			03001233393
The Eve Appeal	Gynae cancer information and support service	eveappeal.org.uk			
Rock my Menopause	Wealth of information, includes trans menopause support	rockmymenopause.com			
The British Menopause Society	find the menopause standards here and links to the NICE guidelines, you'll need for those doctors appointments	thebms.org.uk			
The Daisy Network	POI and premature menopause support	daisynetwork.org	@thedaisynetwork	Daisy Network	
The Samaritans	Mental health and suicide support	samaritans.org			Call free from mobiles: 116 123
The Endometriosis Foundation	Fantastic info, support and campaigning	theendometriosisfoundation.org	@theendometriosisfoundation	The Endometriosis Foundation	
The Hysterectomy Association	Info on surgeries, supporting with choices.	Hysterectomy-association.org.uk			

SOCIAL MEDIA ACCOUNTS I LOVE

@alexlight_london
body positivity

@katerh_fitness
Building strength through strength and community

@dr_naomipotter
She's in the know about HRT

@Amypolly
Mindfullness rebel, not robot!

@knowyourfloors
Work that pelvic floor to banging tunes!

@drnightarif
Womans health advocate, for all stages of our lives, she's got your back.

@a_ray_of_positivity_
Endo warrior with positive words

@lisa_snowdon
Holds regular lives on her peri-meopause journey

@silversheis
Candid vaginal atrophy warrior

@breathpod
Simple breathwork to chilled beats

@luinluland
Her honesty, badass, no fucks given!

@Surgical_menopause_clubuk
always great support and information shared

@diananash
Soulful sounds, healing vibes

@menopause whilstblack
I love learning from Karens account and podcast

@thehappyvagina
so funny, so real and the podcast is great too

@freeda_en
Little revolutionary stories to learn from

@moodswings_and_otherthings
Lotti is a beaut, real life with humour

@womankind collective
Jinty & Lou are total gems, their podcast is my Sunday listen whilst cooking a roast!

@happyplaceofficial
Fearne Cottons community is all round feel good

@mymenopause coach
Knowledgeable on medications/allergies/nutrition

@yourfuturefit
bitesize workouts from someone who get's it!

APPS I LOVE AND USE:

Balance – Fantastic source of information for all types of menopause on the go.

Insight timer – My 'go to' for meditations, uplifting listens and the odd mini course

MapMyRun - keeps me on track of my walks/runs

MindfulnessBell – a simple bell that chimes randomly allowing you to take a moment to breathe

Perry – Across the Atlantic a great community, interesting lives/info

Pinterest - Losing hours to beautiful pics for my vision board

Spotify – Building my playlists from sleep to dancing in my kitchen, to rage!

The Little Extras...   Always Remember You're a Badass Queen!

**HERE IS A SPACE FOR ADDITIONAL
CONTACTS YOU WANT TO HOLD CLOSE:**

Brain Dump

My Goals / Actions

Brain Dump

My Goals / Actions

Brain Dump

The Little Extras...   Always Remember You're a Badass Queen!

My Menopause, My Journal, My Rules!

My Goals / Actions

HERE LIE MY FUCKS THAT I SHALL BURN!

Just watch your fucks go up!

WATCH ME BURN & LET ME GO

just watch your fires go up!

HERE LIE MY FUCKS THAT I SHALL BURN!

just watch your fucks go up!

WATCH ME BURN & LET ME GO

just watch your fuse go up!

HERE LIE MY FUCKS THAT I SHALL BURN!

just watch your fucks go up!

WATCH ME BURN & LET ME GO

just watch your fucks go up!

SCREAM ON A PAGE!

there's zero shame

Give it some on this page, then rip it out and dispose where it is never to be seen again. Let it all go, you'll feel better for it.

ARRRRGGGGHHHHHHH

SCREAM ON A PAGE!

there's zero shame

ARRRRGGGGHHHHHHH

SCREAM ON A PAGE!

there's zero shame

ARRRRGGGGHHHHHHH

SCREAM ON A PAGE!

there's zero shame

ARRRRGGGGHHHHHHH

it's in your hands now...

SO MUCH GRATITUDE...

I might not ever get to do a Bafta speech, so here is me, giving a whole load of thanks for this book becoming a reality...

To my body:

Thank you for being so mighty fine and strong, and to my uterus and ovaries, without you little guys doing one...I wouldn't be here to write the words on the pages!

The kids:

My Sloth-teen and The Boy. Blimey you have put up with a lot. You have made me think beyond myself, to what world there could and should be around talking about this stuff. You ate beans on toast for dinner to fund this and you were patient when I was at my best to write and you still loved me when mental health was not on my side. You are loved oh so much.

Husband:

You believed in me, challenged and reigned me in when needed. This health journey has been ours, you have always been there to hold me up. You are the binding to my pages.

Logan-dog:

Thanks for being my friend in the dark days, for being the reason to walk in nature and for laying on endless coffee shop floors, whilst my fingers typed.

The Folks:

Learning from me as much as I have from you both, you instilled a confidence in me and made me different. I love that I'm different! Thank you.

The Menopause Warriors:

Amy Fleming, Claire Williams, Diane Dizanbrink, Fay Reid, Gayle Stevens-White, Gemma's Dad, Kerry Cameron, Mabel Clifton, Michel Deronzki, Natasha Owens, Pauline Ost, Sam Adams, Sheree Hargreaves, Sophie Lauren. Your openness, vulnerability and willingness to 'go there' with your experiences will help so many. You have bought this alive by creating the connection that as humans we need so much.

Experts in the House:

Amy Polly, Diana Nash, Kim Vopni, Lucienne Shakir, Sam Adams, Tania Nishi; your knowledge inspires me and I'm grateful you shared it with me to pass on. Please keep doing what you are doing.

Dr John, my therapist, I owe you a lot for connecting the dots and encouraging me to find my creativity again.

My faves:

Listening to me harp on about this book for ages, with utter belief in me to make it happen. I'm thankful you've all bought copies (even though you're nowhere near menopause!) leaving raving reviews to boost the algorithm!

Finally to you, the owner of what's within these pages...

Thank you, because it was you I had in mind always. You inspired me to keep going and I hope you have enjoyed making it your own. Your own menopause, your own Journal and your own mighty fine rules!

Please share the love, write a review, I'd massively appreciate it.

Let's keep the conversation rolling.

See ya on the other side!

I'M SHOUTING LOUD ON:

- 🌐 gingeunhinged.com
- 📷 @ginge_unhinged
- ♪ @gingeunhinged